YORKTOWN'S
CIVIL WAR SIEGE

YORKTOWN'S
CIVIL WAR SIEGE

Drums Along the Warwick

JOHN V. QUARSTEIN
AND J. MICHAEL MOORE

THE
History
PRESS

Published by The History Press
Charleston, SC 29403
www.historypress.net

Copyright © 2012 by John V. Quarstein and J. Michael Moore
All rights reserved

Cover image: Battle of Dam No. 1, oil on panel, Sidney King, 1962. *Courtesy of the Newport News Collection.*

First published 2012
Second printing 2013

Manufactured in the United States

ISBN 978.1.60949.656.2

Library of Congress CIP data applied for.

To Our Fathers
Colonel Vernon Alfred Quarstein, USA (Ret.), PhD
and
James Marvin Moore

These men, in their own ways, served their nation well during war and peace. Following their military service, they both became educators and sought to share their vast knowledge with others. Their sense of duty, quest for excellence and committment to community gave me and Michael the wherewithal to create this volume. As an expression of the highest appreciation for who these men were, it is our privilege to dedicate Yorktown's Civil War Siege: Drums Along the Warwick *to them. Our fathers have gone to a brighter place where trials and tribulations do not come, yet thankfully their legacies will always remain with us.*

—John V. Quarstein
8 June 2012

Contents

Acknowledgments

This book has actually been percolating in my head for over fifteen years. It is the culmination of all my scholarship, story-telling and preservation efforts during the past two decades. This tale is all about numerous sites that I have helped preserve and present: Lee Hall Mansion, Lee's Mill and Young's Mill, Endview Plantation, the Williamsburg Battlefield and Fort Monroe.

Since most of these preservation achievements were accomplished in the city of Newport News, Virginia, where I worked for over thirty years as the director of the Virginia War Museum, I must thank Ronnie Burroughs and Michael Poplawski, both of whom served as director of Newport News Parks, Recreation and Tourism, for all their support of my writing about Newport News history, as well as for aiding in the preservation of Civil War sites like Lee Hall Mansion. Thanks to their encouragement, the history in this volume can still be seen and enjoyed today.

J. Michael Moore is my co-author for *Yorktown's Civil War Siege: Drums Along the Warwick*. Michael and I have worked together for nearly fifteen years, and he has assisted me with my previous books. Not only have we been colleagues over these years, but he has also become a very good friend and great duck hunting partner. I so wanted Michael to help me write this book because he has several ancestors who served in the 15th North Carolina during the Battle of Dam No. 1. Sergeant John Thomas Dillard was wounded in action by a ball to the head at this battle on 16 April 1862. John Dillard served along the Warwick River with his brothers, Sergeant James Henry Dillard and

Lee Hall Mansion, Newport News, Virginia, circa 1938. *Courtesy of the Library of Virginia.*

Private Edward Dillard. Michael's family connections made my working on this volume and being on the battlefield with him ever more meaningful.

My thanks must also go out to Julie Murphy for editing this volume, the fifth that we have worked on together. Once again, Julie's excellent writing and editing skills truly enhance my style and presentation of this powerful history. Special thanks also to Julie's mother, Anne Bobbitt Murphy, for providing documentation for several ancestors who served in the defense of the Peninsula and especially for the papers of Captain Vines E. Turner of the 23rd North Carolina. Turner, then a 2nd lieutenant, fought at the Battle of Williamsburg, serving in Early's brigade. He participated in the desperate attack through the Custis wheat field to strike at Winfield Scott Hancock's brigade at Redoubt #11 on 5 May 1862. He somehow survived that bloody field and faithfully continued to serve his cause until Appomattox, writing truly compelling letters that provide great insights into the first phase of the Peninsula Campaign. Julie's great-great-grandfather, William A. Blackley, fought at Dam No. 1, serving as corporal in Company E, North Carolina 15th Infantry, the same regiment as Michael's ancestors.

There are just so many others to thank and who are due my appreciation for supporting this book. Anthony McCarron and Jenn Hesse helped type the text. My friend Kimberlee, Jenn's mother, offered friendly support that enabled me to focus on providing this thorough account of the days when the drums beat along the Warwick.

My son, John Moran, has an ancestor, 1st Lieutenant William B. Jones of the Peninsula Artillery, 1st Virginia Artillery, who fought at Lee's Mill on 5 April 1862. He has several other Harwood ancestors who served in the Warwick Beauregards of the 32nd Virginia Regiment. John Moran provided many of the images found in this book. Other prints, photos and paintings that illustrate this volume are from the collections of Lee Hall Mansion, The Mariners' Museum, Casemate Museum, Virginia War Museum, Virginia Historical Society and the Library of Virginia.

Michael and I decided to dedicate this book about the Peninsula Campaign to our fathers. Shortly after we began working on the text in the fall of 2010, Michael's father, James Marvin Moore, died after a long illness. Likewise, my father, Colonel Vernon A. Quarstein, USA (Ret.), PhD, USMA, class of 1950, also died early in 2012 after being ill far too long. Our fathers were both educators. Michael's father taught physics and mathematics at

Edward (in both left and right images) and Mary Morgan Dillard. *Courtesy of Robert Dillard Mallison.*

Acknowledgments

Newport News Shipbuilding's Apprentice School, whereas my father, after his retirement from the U.S. Army, received his PhD in finance and taught at Hampton University, Old Dominion University and Saint Leo University. We learned a great deal from their knowledge and experience. Accordingly, we proudly dedicate *Yorktown's Civil War Siege: Drums Along the Warwick* to their memory. Our fathers were truly outstanding individuals who gave each of us the wherewithal to achieve positive actions that continue to contribute to our community.

—*John V. Quarstein*
Historian, city of Newport News

Introduction

The spring of 1862 was a dark time for the Confederacy. Defeats had come on the Mississippi River, in Tennessee and along the Carolina coast. A powerful Union army was poised outside Washington, D.C., ready to strike a blow against Richmond, the Confederate capital. The events that took place that spring along the rivers, swamps and fields of the Virginia Peninsula were initiated to do just that—capture Richmond and end the war.

The Peninsula Campaign was the strategic concept of Major General George Brinton McClellan. By advancing up the Peninsula, McClellan would avoid suffering the high casualties caused by a march south from northern Virginia. McClellan's concept relied on the Union navy to transport his army to the Peninsula. Then the Federal fleet would use the James and York Rivers to protect the Army of the Potomac's flanks and carry its supplies as the Federals marched up the Peninsula toward Richmond. It was an excellent plan, and McClellan's army seemed unstoppable. Yet despite all these advantages, he failed to achieve his goals, in many ways due to the events that occurred in the Hampton Roads region.

The story actually began on 17 April 1861, when Virginia left the Union. The Hampton Roads region contained some of America's greatest military assets, including Fort Monroe on Old Point Comfort and the Gosport Navy Yard across the Elizabeth River from Norfolk. Fort Monroe was never threatened by the Confederates. The Southerners lacked a navy, heavy siege guns and adequate manpower to threaten Union control of this powerful coastal fort. The fort was immediately reinforced and would remain the key to Union control of the lower Chesapeake Bay. Despite this circumstance, the Confederates acted quickly to force the Federals to abandon Gosport on 20 April 1861. The capture of the largest navy yard in America gave the Confederacy the capability of challenging Union control of the entrance to Hampton Roads.

The Confederates needed time, but it appeared in May 1861 that the luxury of time would not be afforded them. As the U.S. Navy probed the fledgling Confederate defenses guarding the York and Elizabeth Rivers, a new Union commander arrived on the Peninsula: Major General Benjamin Franklin Butler. Along with Butler, thousands of new Union recruits were arriving on the Peninsula, and many more were en route. Butler, therefore, immediately began to flex Union power. On 23 May 1861, the Union general sent the 1st Vermont Volunteers into the nearby town of Hampton to close the polls, as that day the Virginians were to vote on the Ordinance of Secession. The Vermonters closed the polls and returned to Camp Hamilton outside of Fort Monroe. This brief occupation of Hampton prompted three slaves to run away and enter Union lines. Butler proclaimed them "Contraband of War," and very quickly, hundreds of African Americans were seeking refuge. General Butler, however, was more intent on expanding the Union position up the Peninsula toward Richmond. On 27 May 1861, Union troops occupied Newport News Point and established Camp Butler. This action closed the riverine link between Norfolk and Richmond. Hampton was abandoned by Confederate soldiers and civilians.

As the refugees streamed up the Peninsula toward Williamsburg, many were met by Colonel John Bankhead Magruder. "Prince John," as he was fondly called for his flamboyant lifestyle, had just been assigned as commander of the Department of the Peninsula, and he vowed vengeance on the Federals for their expansion into Southern territory. The Confederate commander realized that he needed time to prepare an effective defensive system. Accordingly, he established a forward position at Big Bethel to bait Butler to attack the Confederate fortifications. Butler complied. On 10 June 1861, the Federals struck at Big Bethel with a poorly organized advance and were repulsed. Big Bethel was the Civil War's first land battle and made John Bankhead Magruder one of the South's first heroes. As more Confederate reinforcements arrived on the Peninsula, Magruder became more aggressive. While several skirmishes occurred along the Hampton Road, Magruder's command reached all the way to Camp Butler on 6 August where the Confederates discovered a New York newspaper reporting that the Federals intended to use the abandoned town of Hampton to house Union soldiers and contrabands. Consequently, Magruder ordered the town destroyed. Local Confederate soldiers burned their hometown on 7 August 1861.

Meanwhile, Magruder initiated the construction of three defensive lines across the Peninsula to counter the Union positions on the tip of the Peninsula. Forward positions (known as the First Peninsula defensive line) at Young's Mill, Big Bethel, Howard's Bridge and Ship's Point on the Poquoson River enabled the Confederates to maintain their security and send troops to harass Federal soldiers foraging from their fortifications below Newmarket Creek. The main Confederate defensive system was the Warwick-Yorktown Line. This line reached along the Warwick River from Mulberry Island Point to Yorktown. Additional riverine flank protection was secured by Fort Huger and Fort Boykin on the south side of the James River and Gloucester Point on the north side of the York River. This twelve-mile-long line of earthworks was supported by a series of fourteen redoubts sited between College and Queen's Creeks known as the Williamsburg Line. Magruder used more than 600 slaves per day and soldiers from his command to construct these defenses. By early March 1862, Magruder and his 13,000-man command were ready to contest any Union advance.

Following the Union defeat at First Manassas on 27 July 1861, President Abraham Lincoln named Major General McClellan as commander of the Army of the Potomac. Eventually, McClellan would be named general-in-chief of the Union army. As Magruder built earthworks, McClellan forged the Army of the Potomac into the largest and best-equipped army yet to be witnessed on the North American continent. McClellan, however, hesitated to launch it into battle until President Lincoln forced him to develop a plan of action. His initial plan was an advance against Richmond by way of Urbanna on the Rappahannock River. This would have placed the Union army behind General Joseph E. Johnston's Confederate army, then positioned in northern Virginia. When Johnston withdrew farther south to Fredericksburg from the Manassas Line beginning on 6 March 1862, McClellan had to scrap his original plan and select his second alternative, the Peninsula. McClellan believed that by using Fort Monroe as a base, he could march against Richmond and capture the Confederate capital.

Just as McClellan shared the merits of his plan with President Lincoln, the plan started to unhinge. The emergence of the ironclad ram the CSS *Virginia* (*Merrimack*) on 8 March sent shock waves through the Union command. In one day, the *Virginia* destroyed two Union warships, the USS *Congress* and USS *Cumberland*, threatening Union control of Hampton

Roads. A strategic balance was quickly gained when the novel Union ironclad USS *Monitor* arrived and fought the *Virginia* to a standstill the next day. While both sides claimed victory, the *Virginia*'s presence denied the Federals use of the James River.

Confident that the *Monitor* could hold off any advance against his transports by the Confederate ironclad, McClellan proceeded with his campaign. He began shipping his huge army, with all of its supplies and armaments, to Fort Monroe on 17 March 1862, intending to move against Richmond by way of the York River. On 4 April, McClellan's army began its march up the Peninsula. The next day, the Army of the Potomac found its path to Richmond slowed at first by heavy rains and then blocked by Magruder's "Army of the Peninsula" behind the Warwick River. As McClellan carefully surveyed the extensive Confederate fortifications, "Prince John" Magruder paraded his troops along the earthworks, deluding the Union commander into believing that he was outnumbered.

The events of 5 April changed McClellan's campaign. His plans for a rapid movement past Yorktown against Richmond were upset not only by the unexpected Confederate defenses but also by Lincoln's decision not to release elements of Major General Irvin McDowell's I Corps from northern Virginia to use on a flanking movement against the Confederate batteries at Gloucester Point. President Abraham Lincoln had demoted McClellan from general-in-chief to commander of the Army of the Potomac. Lincoln, as commander-in-chief, wished to hold the I Corps for the defense of Washington, D.C., as well as to support Union operations in the Shenandoah Valley against Major General Thomas J. "Stonewall" Jackson. The U.S. Navy, too, refused to attempt any offensive action in the York River because of the CSS *Virginia*. Since McClellan's reconnaissance (provided by detective Allan Pinkerton's and Professor Thaddeus Lowe's balloons) confirmed his belief that he was outnumbered by the Confederates, the Union commander thought that he had no choice but to besiege the Confederate defenses.

As his men built gun emplacements for the 101 siege guns that McClellan had brought to the Peninsula, General Joseph E. Johnston was ordered to take his entire Confederate army from Fredericksburg to the Lower Peninsula. Johnston believed that Magruder's position was weak, noting that "[n]o one but McClellan could have hesitated to attack." McClellan's men did make one effort to break the Warwick-Yorktown Line. Brigadier General William Smith sent elements of the Vermont brigade across the Warwick River to disrupt Confederate control of Dam No. 1. The poorly coordinated assaults on 16 April 1862 failed to break through the vulnerable Confederate position.

The siege continued another two weeks, even though Johnston counseled retreat. Johnston advised President Jefferson Davis that "the fight for Yorktown must be one of artillery, in which we cannot win." Finally, just as McClellan made his last preparations to unleash his heavy bombardment on the Confederate lines, Johnston abandoned the Warwick-Yorktown Line on 3 May.

When the Confederate army left its fortifications, the troops were never to return to the Peninsula. The retreat would have immediate repercussions. Norfolk was isolated, and this left the Gosport Navy Yard and the CSS *Virginia* at risk. Even though McClellan rapidly reacted to the Confederate retreat, he failed to destroy Johnston's army. The Union army struck at the Confederate rear guard along the Williamsburg Line on 4 and 5 May in an inconclusive action. McClellan also tried to cut off the Confederate retreat to Richmond at Eltham's Landing; however, this action did not achieve any success. President Lincoln, frustrated by McClellan's lack of progress, had already arrived at Fort Monroe on 6 May. Lincoln orchestrated Norfolk's capture on 10 May. The *Virginia*, left without a port and with too great of a draft to steam to Richmond, was scuttled by her own crew. The James River was open all the way to Drewry's Bluff, eight miles below Richmond. More importantly, all of Hampton Roads was firmly under Union control.

The siege of Yorktown had far-reaching implications. McClellan's hesitation in front of Magruder's defenses gave the Confederacy time to mobilize its forces for an effective defense of Richmond. Although McClellan should have taken advantage of several weak points in the Confederate defensive line, he never made a decisive effort to do so. The Peninsula Campaign's first phase was a failure in combined operations for both North and South. The Federals had successfully used their naval superiority in cooperation with their field armies to inflict serious defeats on the Confederacy. The team of Brigadier General Ulysses Grant and Flag Officer Andrew Foote is the best example. These two officers joined together to capture Fort Donelson and Fort Henry in Tennessee. Union gunboats were also on hand to save the Union army at Shiloh. McClellan understood combined operations, and his campaign strategy, as well as its success, rested on working in concert with the U.S. Navy. Flag Officer Louis M. Goldsborough was simply intimidated by the CSS *Virginia*. Goldsborough, despite his superiority in ships, would not try to combat the Confederate ironclad, refused to operate in the James River and failed to attack the Confederate batteries defending the York River.

Union occupation of Yorktown. *Courtesy of the Virginia War Museum.*

McClellan, believing his army outnumbered by the Confederate army on the Peninsula, felt that his only option was siege. Joe Johnston realized that his army could never withstand the Union bombardment and abandoned the Peninsula. His retreat, however, had tragic implications for the Confederacy.

Magruder did not understand the *Virginia*'s power and refused to cooperate with Flag Officer Franklin Buchanan in the attack on Newport News Point. More importantly, Johnston refused to recognize the *Virginia*'s importance to the defense of Richmond. He and Benjamin Huger failed to give the Confederate navy the time it needed to take its ironclad to Richmond. Nevertheless, despite the loss of Norfolk, the CSS *Virginia* and the vast agricultural resources of the Hampton Roads region, Richmond would be saved because the Confederate soldiers and sailors lived to fight another day. *Sic, transit Gloria, Peninsula.*

Union Outpost

As the secession crisis began to spread throughout the South, Brevet Lieutenant General Winfield Scott immediately recognized the need to make secure several Southern coastal defense forts. Scott, a hero of the War of 1812 and the Mexican War, had been general-in-chief of the U.S. Army since 1841. He realized that certain forts could be retained if properly reinforced. Fort Monroe, guarding the lower Chesapeake Bay and the entrance to Hampton Roads, was one of the most important installations in the South. Built between 1819 and 1834, Fort Monroe was the largest moat-encircled stone fortification in North America. The fort was designed to mount 412 heavy guns with a wartime garrison of 2,625 officers and men. A companion fortification, Fort Calhoun, was built on the Rip Raps Shoal to complete control of the harbor entrance. Even though these fortifications appeared formidable, Fort Calhoun was incomplete and unmanned and Fort Monroe's garrison was not up to strength.

Scott felt secure about Fort Monroe regardless of what Virginia might do if war erupted. His confidence in the fort and its commander, Lieutenant Colonel Justin Dimick, was complete. Dimick, an 1819 West Point graduate from Connecticut, was a forty-two-year veteran brevetted for gallantry during the Seminole and Mexican Wars. He was well aware of the rising threats to the Union control of Hampton Roads and acted to strengthen Fort Monroe's defenses by mounting additional cannons. When Virginia did secede on 17 April 1861, no effort was made to capture the fort. The Confederates simply lacked the resources to besiege the fort or otherwise take it by treachery. Dimick had been mindful of his officers' loyalty. Furthermore, the Confederates just did not have sufficient men, heavy cannons or ships to block any Union effort to reinforce the fort. Consequently, on 20 April, the fort received its first reinforcements when the 3rd and 4th Massachusetts regiments arrived at Old Point Comfort by steamer.

General Scott had also detailed Captain Horatio G. Wright, "an engineer officer of high science and judgement,"[1] to support Union operations defending Gosport Navy Yard. Gosport was the largest navy yard in America, and the Confederates were determined to capture it. Unfortunately for the Union, the yard's commandant in April 1861 was Flag Officer Charles Stewart McCauley. The sixty-seven-year-old veteran was considered by many to be too old for command. Rumors about his drinking were rampant. Thirteen of his twenty officers would eventually join the Confederacy—consequently, much of the advice he received was tempered by questionable loyalties. McCauley was under tremendous pressure. Union Secretary of the Navy Gideon Welles urged the yard's commandant to do everything he could to defend the yard and get the steam-screw frigate USS *Merrimack* ready for sea; however, Welles also told McCauley not to upset the Virginians, and he left everything to the flag officer's discretion.

Meanwhile, Virginia Militia Major General William Booth Taliaferro surrounded the yard and demanded Gosport's return to the Commonwealth of Virginia. On 19 April, Taliaferro's volunteers captured Fort Norfolk, across the Elizabeth River from the yard, placed obstructions in the river and began shuttling trains in and out of Portsmouth using the same troops to give the appearance of greater strength. These actions unnerved McCauley even further. Although Chief Engineer Benjamin Franklin Isherwood had the *Merrimack*'s condemned engines operating, McCauley refused to allow the frigate to leave the yard on 19 April. Isherwood reported this circumstance to Gideon Welles, and Welles organized a task force under the command of Flag Officer Hiram Paulding to take over the yard from McCauley.

Paulding left the Washington Navy Yard aboard the eight-gun steamer USS *Pawnee* with a force of 100 marines. This task force arrived at Old Point Comfort on the afternoon of 20 April. There, Captain Wright loaded combustibles and 350 men from the 3rd Massachusetts. This regiment had just arrived at Fort Monroe and was commanded by Colonel David W. Wardrop. By the time Paulding's relief force reached Gosport, it was too late. McCauley had already ordered the yard abandoned and destroyed. Every major warship in the harbor was on fire except the sloop of war *Cumberland* and the venerable frigate *United States*. The scene was made even more eerie as darkness came. The fire reached the guns of the huge ship of the line *Pennsylvania*, and they randomly exploded. All Paulding could do was to continue McCauley's destructive work. The Federals left the yard in apparent ruins before dawn. The *Pawnee* towed the *Cumberland*, followed by the gunboat *Yankee*. By 6:15 a.m., these ships had anchored off Fort Monroe and initiated the Union blockade of Hampton Roads.

Despite all their efforts, the Federals had not completely destroyed the yard. When the Confederates entered the yard, they quickly discovered that most of the yard's vast resources—including the foundry, the machine shop, the granite dry dock, tons of supplies, 1,085 heavy cannons, 110,217 artillery projectiles, 154,605 percussion caps, 158,467 small-arms cartridges and 250,000 pounds of gunpowder—were available for the Confederacy's use. Besides all of this equipment and weaponry, three warships—*Merrimack*, *Germantown* and *Plymouth*—could be salvaged. The Richmond press gloated over the abundance of material and supplies: "We have enough to build a navy of iron-plated ships."[2]

The Confederacy may have gained the wherewithal to build a navy when Gosport was captured, but the Union's ability to retain Fort Monroe firmly closed the door on Confederate commerce leaving Hampton Roads. Immediately the Union navy enforced the blockade and used Hampton Roads as the anchorage for the newly created North Atlantic Blockading Squadron. Dimick called for more reinforcements, and Scott sent as many new regiments as were available. On the same day that Wardrop's 3rd Massachusetts arrived at Fort Monroe, so did Colonel Abner B. Packard's 4th Massachusetts Regiment. Scott was pleased to write to Dimick that "Fort Monroe is by far the most secure post now in possession of the U.S., against any attack that can be possibly made upon it, independent of the War Vessels, the *Cumberland* and the *Niagara*, at hand, and approaching you."[3] Fort Monroe continued to receive reinforcements. On 13 May, Colonel John Wolcott Phelps's 1st Vermont Regiment arrived, along with two additional companies of the 3rd Massachusetts. These additional troops necessitated that on the next day Dimick occupy the Segar and Clark farms across Mill Creek Bridge in Elizabeth City County. Fort Monroe was overcrowded and lacked the fresh water and sanitation system to support all these reinforcements. The new Union encampment, which was protected by Fort Monroe's heavy artillery, was first called Camp Troy but was quickly renamed Camp Hamilton. It was the first occupation of Southern territory during the war.

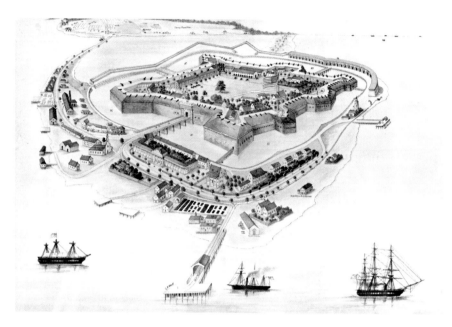

Fort Monroe, Old Point Comfort, Virginia, 1862. *Courtesy of John Moran Quarstein.*

The expanding Union strength on the Peninsula prompted Winfield Scott to send a higher-ranking officer to command the newly created Union Department of Virginia. Scott selected one of the Civil War's most unusual and controversial generals, Major General Benjamin Franklin Butler, to assume command of the Union Department of Virginia, headquartered at Fort Monroe. Butler's orders entailed that the newly promoted major general disrupt and capture enemy batteries within a half day's march of Fort Monroe, as well as threaten or capture Craney Island and Gosport Navy Yard. As soon as Butler arrived at Fort Monroe aboard the Old Bay Line steamer *Adelaide* on 22 May, he began to broaden the Union toehold on the Peninsula.

Ben Butler was a cockeyed and corpulent yet astute criminal lawyer and prewar Democratic politician from Massachusetts. Butler had already achieved instant fame during the conflict's first days when he thwarted the Maryland secessionist movement following the 19 April Baltimore Riot. His actions occupying that prewar slave state under Union control gave him immediate notoriety. Accordingly, Butler recognized that his new assignment offered him opportunities for even greater glory.

On 23 May 1861, Butler decided to break the informal truce that existed between the Federal and Confederate forces on the Peninsula. He ordered

Colonel Phelps, an 1836 West Point graduate and ardent abolitionist, into the town of Hampton to disrupt the Ordinance of Secession vote that was to occur that day. Other than the Confederate failure to burn the Hampton Creek Bridge to block the Union approach, the Vermonters' march in and out of Hampton was without event. Nevertheless, amid all the confusion, three slaves—Shephard Mallory, James Townsend and Fred Baker—went to Fort Monroe to secure their freedom. When the slaves' owner, Colonel Charles King Mallory, sent Major John Baytop Cary to retrieve his property, Butler declared these men to be "Contraband of War." Ben Butler's Contraband of War decision began the war's transition into a conflict to end slavery. Soon hundreds of African Americans were escaping into Union lines.

Major General Benjamin Franklin Butler, USA. *Courtesy of the Library of Congress.*

Butler had not come to Virginia to end slavery; rather, his goal was to expand the Union presence toward Richmond. On 27 May, Butler sent three regiments under the overall command of Colonel Phelps aboard the steamer USS *Pawnee* to occupy Newport News Point. The Federals immediately began building an entrenched camp known as Camp Butler. This position included a water battery mounting four 8-inch Columbiads. Butler reported to Winfield Scott that the new position closed the James River to Confederate riverine traffic and could be used to strike at Suffolk, thereby cutting Norfolk's railroad link with Richmond.

The Federals were testing Confederate positions everywhere in Hampton Roads. The USS *Yankee* had previously shelled Gloucester Point on 7 May only to receive return fire from the recently arrived 2nd Company, Richmond Howitzers. As soon as the Confederates had captured Gosport Navy Yard, the yard's commandant, Flag Officer French Forrest, initiated an effort to defend the Elizabeth River. Virginia Militia Major General Walter Gwynn, an 1822 West Point graduate and internationally recognized railroad engineer, organized the construction

Building earthworks at Camp Butler, Newport News, Virginia. *Courtesy of the Virginia War Museum.*

of batteries at Sewell's Point and Craney Island. These fortifications were nearing completion when Union gunboats shelled Sewell's Point on 18 and 19 May 1861. Federal sea power and expanding Union troop strength on the tip of the Peninsula meant that the entire region could fall under Union control unless a concerted effort was made to block the Federals' movement up the Peninsula.

Major Benjamin Stoddert Ewell, president of the College of William and Mary and an 1832 graduate of West Point, was doing everything in his power to stem any Union advance. The job was overwhelming, and Ewell did not appear to be totally up to the task. Consequently, on 21 May 1861, Major General Robert E. Lee, then commander of the Provisional Army of Virginia, ordered Colonel John Bankhead Magruder to assume command of the troops and military operations on the line to Hampton and instructed him to establish his headquarters at Yorktown. Magruder, a hero of the Mexican War, arrived at Yorktown on board the steamer *Logan.* Magruder quickly set himself to the enormous task of organizing troops and fortifications on the Peninsula. He immediately began bombarding Richmond with requests for troops, armaments and supplies. His first report noted that "I shall need at least four companies of cavalry to operate against the advance of troops against Hampton, to cut off their parties, to harass

Map of the Lower Peninsula. *Courtesy of John Moran Quarstein.*

them on the march, and beat up their quarters at night."[4] The Confederate Peninsula commander also wrote:

> *When I took command there were no works on the James River below Jamestown, no fortifications at Williamsburg, Yorktown or Gloucester Point, with the exception of one gun at Yorktown and perhaps two at Gloucester Point. I had to defend a Peninsula 90 miles in length and some 10 miles in width, enclosed between two navigable rivers, terminated by fortresses impregnable as long as the enemy commanded the waters.*
>
> *I...made a tour on horseback of the lower part of the Peninsula, in order to get some knowledge of the country. Seeing at a glance that three broad rivers could not be defended without fortifications, and that these never could be built if the enemy knew our weakness and want of preparation, I determined to display a portion of my small force in his immediate presence, and forthwith selected Bethel as a place at which a small force could best give him battle should he advise.*
>
> *Returning to Yorktown, I called upon Mr. R.D. Lee, who had mills on that stream, to show one the line of the Warwick River, which rises near Yorktown, flows across the country, and enters James River a little below Mulberry Point, where there is now a fort. Having made this exploration, I determined to adopt this line to Mulberry Point as the true line of defense whenever its right flank, of James River, could be protected by water batteries.[5]*

Magruder believed that with twenty-five thousand men arrayed along his proposed Warwick-Yorktown Line, he could hold off the advance of any enemy force. What Magruder needed was time and men. He was anxious to begin work on his main defensive line and ordered Benjamin Stoddert Ewell to focus on constructing the Williamsburg defensive line. Before he could establish any defensive presence, refugees began streaming up the Peninsula. Most of the residents of Hampton abandoned their homes when the Federals established Camp Butler on Newport News Point. This exodus of civilians up the Peninsula and Butler's aggressive movements had pushed the Federal lines to Newmarket Creek.

Butler continued to receive reinforcements throughout late May and early June 1861. Several elite units, such as the 5th New York (also known as Duryee's Zouaves), arrived on the Peninsula. These men increased Butler's troop strength and emboldened the Federals. During the first week of June, the Federals marched to Fox Hill and skirmishers ranged as far as Big

Colonel Benjamin Stoddert Ewell, CSA.
Courtesy of the Museum of the Confederacy.

Bethel Church. There, at the crossing of the northwest branch of the Back River (also referred to as Brick Kiln Creek or Wythe Creek), elements of Duryee's Zouaves defaced the sides of the church with graffiti stating "Down with the Rebels!" and "Death to the Traitors!!" The U.S. Navy also continued to probe the Confederate water batteries. The USS *Harriet Lane* shelled the Pig Point Battery at the mouth of the Nansemond River, directly across Hampton Roads from Camp Butler. The Confederate battery, commanded by Captain Robert Pegram, CSN, was able to drive the Union gunboat off.

Magruder, meanwhile, was also on the move. He had received reinforcements, bringing his overall troop strength up to 2,500 men. The new units arriving at Yorktown included Colonel Daniel Harvey Hill's 1st North Carolina Regiment, Major Edgar Montague's Virginia Battalion and additional companies of Major George Wythe Randolph's Richmond Howitzers. Magruder realized that he must give his small army time to build his main defensive line without interference from the Federals. Accordingly, he decided to go on the offensive and selected an advance position at Big Bethel Church where the Hampton-York Road (also referred to as Sawyer Swamp Road) crossed Brick Kiln Creek.

On 6 June, Magruder sent troops to establish a fortified position at Big Bethel. The main earthwork was built around the church. A smaller battery was built on the south side of the creek to command the road's approach to the bridge. Eventually, the Confederate force would number 1,404 men, including the 1st North Carolina, four companies of the 3rd (later redesignated the 15th) Virginia Infantry, Montague's Virginia Battalion, the Wythe Rifles and two companies of the Richmond Howitzers. Magruder also supported these units with two companies of cavalry commanded by Major John Bell Hood.

Once the Confederate position had been firmly established, Magruder sent elements of the 1st North Carolina to Little Bethel and beyond to reconnoiter Union strength. On 7 and 9 June, Federal units clashed with

Brigadier General John Bell Hood, CSA.
Courtesy of the Museum of the Confederacy.

these Confederates between Little Bethel and Newmarket Creek Bridge. Butler was now alert to the Confederate presence near Hampton that threatened communications between Fort Monroe and Camp Butler. Reports of the Confederate outpost at Little Bethel and fortifications at Big Bethel convinced the Union general that he must attack them. The capture of Big Bethel, Butler believed, would open the door to Richmond. Therefore, Butler, with the assistance of his military secretary Major Theodore Winthrop, conceived a complex plan to send troops from Camp Hamilton, Camp Butler and Fort Monroe to converge near Little Bethel before dawn on 10 June. The night march was planned to give the Union force an element of surprise that, it was hoped, would ensure victory.

The Union strike force was placed under the command of Massachusetts Brigadier General Ebenezer Weaver Peirce. The general was ordered to capture and burn both Bethels. The Duryee's Zouaves, with one howitzer, led the advance from Camp Hamilton; the 3rd New York followed. Lieutenant Peter T. Washburn of the 1st Vermont organized men from his own regiment and the 4th Massachusetts into the New England Battalion. Washburn's men were followed by the 7th New York (also called the Steuben Regiment) and two howitzers commanded by Lieutenant John Trout Greble of the 2nd U.S. Artillery. These troops from Camp Butler were to juncture with the troops marching from Camp Hamilton near Little Bethel. The Union strike force totaled 4,400 men.

The night march required that the troops wear white armbands and use the password "Boston." Unfortunately, when the 3rd New York and 7th New York approached each other, the Steuben Regiment (which was composed of German-speaking immigrants) fired into the ranks of their fellow New Yorkers. The Union incurred eighteen casualties in the confusion. Even though the Federals became disorganized by the Civil War's first friendly fire incident, Peirce decided to continue the advance.

Meanwhile, Magruder had organized a strike force of nine hundred men from the 1st North Carolina and began to march toward Little Bethel. As they headed down the road, a middle-aged woman named Hannah Nicholson Tunnell stopped the column and warned of the approach of the oncoming four thousand Federals. Magruder ordered his men back to Big Bethel to await the Union attack.

At about 9:00 a.m., the Federals began to reach the battlefield and were thrown into confusion by a shell fired by Major Randolph. An artillery duel ensued between Greble's Artillery and the Richmond Howitzers. The Duryee's Zouaves and New England Battalion made some piecemeal assaults—all were easily repulsed by the Confederates. Peirce somehow regained his composure and organized a concerted attack by the Duryee's Zouaves and 3rd New York against the one-gun battery. Just as the Zouaves neared the redoubt, a priming wire broke in the vent, rendering the howitzer useless. The Confederates fell back across the creek. Unfortunately for the Federals, Colonel Frederick Townsend of the 3rd New York mistook some of his own men as the enemy attempting a flank attack and ordered a retreat. The Duryee's Zouaves were isolated in the battery and forced to fall back just as D.H. Hill organized a counterattack with the Edgecombe Guards of the 1st North Carolina that retook the battery.

As the New Yorkers retreated, Major Theodore Winthrop organized an attack on the left flank of the main Confederate redoubt with the New England Battalion supported by the 7th New York. The Union soldiers crossed the creek at a ford with a loud cheer and rushed the Confederate earthwork. When this initial attack faltered, Winthrop endeavored to rally his men for a final charge. He stood up on a log, waving his sword and shouting, "Come on boys; one charge and the day is ours."[6] He was immediately shot through the heart and fell dead onto the ground. Winthrop's death demoralized his troops, and they retired from the field.

Peirce realized that the day was lost and ordered a retreat. Greble attempted to cover the withdraw with his artillery; however, he was killed by a final cannon shot fired by the Richmond Howitzers. Magruder ordered his cavalry in pursuit, causing some Federals to throw down their equipment and run.

Big Bethel was a complete failure for the Federals. The Union lost a total of seventy-six men: eighteen killed, fifty-three wounded and three missing. This ineptitude required that a scapegoat be found. Butler was blamed for sending his troops forward with such poor intelligence and for remaining at Fort Monroe during the battle. General Peirce, however, took most of

Major General Daniel Harvey Hill, CSA. *Courtesy of the Virginia War Museum.*

the responsibility for the defeat. He was labeled incompetent and mustered out of the army. The Northern press attempted to salvage some honor and called the Union soldiers courageous "as they fought both friend and foe alike with equal resolution."[7]

Southerners rejoiced over the Big Bethel victory. Confederate casualties were light—only one killed and nine wounded. Private Henry Lawson

Wyatt of Company A, Edgecombe Guards, 1ˢᵗ North Carolina, achieved martyrdom as he was the first Confederate enlisted man to be killed in battle. John Bankhead Magruder, nevertheless, was accorded most of the glory for the Big Bethel victory. "He's the hero for our times," one ballad proclaimed, "the furious fighting Johnny B. Magruder."[8] Exactly one week following the battle, on 17 June 1861, Magruder was promoted to brigadier general. The fame seemed to fall on Magruder naturally, and in every fashion he strove to live up to the honor bestowed on him. He was a vigorous fifty-one years old, tall, erect and handsome. Always perfectly uniformed, he appeared magnificently everywhere at a gallop, talking incessantly despite his unusual lisp. His impressive nature, dramatic flair and strategic sense had given the South its first victory.

Lieutenant Baker Perkins Lee of Montague's Battalion observed Magruder before the battle and called him a "picturesque figure," noting that

> [h]e had a fondness for tinsel and tassels. With an irrepressible spirit of restless energy, instinctively susceptible of the charm of danger, full of health and physical force, it was evident that nature made him a soldier… it was in the field, in full military array, well mounted, as he always was, with the fire of patriotic ambition and personal pride in his eye, that he was seen at his best.[9]

While Baker Lee looked upon Magruder as a hero, his prewar army career had not endeared him to everyone. Born in Port Royal, Virginia, on 1 May 1807, he attended the University of Virginia in 1825. The following year, he received an appointment to West Point and graduated fifteen in the class of 1830. Initially assigned to the infantry, Magruder secured a transfer to the artillery in 1831, thanks in part to the support of his uncle, Colonel James Bankhead. He saw service during the Second Seminole War and on the Canadian border during the minor border dispute known as the Aroostook War. Promotions were slow for Magruder until he achieved his first rise to fame during the Mexican War. Captain Magruder commanded Company I, 1ˢᵗ U.S. Artillery, as part of Winfield Scott's advance against Mexico City. Although wounded twice during the assault on Chapultepec, his brilliant use of light artillery tactics helped to foil the Mexican attempt to repulse the American attack. Colonel William S. Harney reported that "Captain Magruder's gallantry was conspicuously displayed on several occasions."[10] His dynamic leadership prompted comments from many, like this note from Lieutenant Thomas J. Jackson: "I wanted to see active service, to be near the enemy and in the fight; and when I heard that John Magruder had his battery, I bent all of my energies to be with him, for I knew if any fighting was to be done Magruder would be on hand."[11] Magruder was brevetted lieutenant colonel for his actions and was awarded a gold sword by the Commonwealth of Virginia.

The secession crisis found Magruder stationed with his battery in Washington. He was still a brevet lieutenant colonel and had spent the last decade serving in California, Texas, Kansas and Rhode Island. A fellow officer, Captain Edward C. Boynton, wrote of Magruder that he was "ambitious, unscrupulous, treacherous, and dissolute, he had one good quality at least—he was a dashing fearless soldier."[12] The antebellum era had not been kind to John Bankhead Magruder. His marriage to the wealthy Baltimore heiress Henrietta von Kapff had fallen apart. Nevertheless, Magruder continued to be a social lion, especially when assigned to Fort Adams, near Newport, Rhode Island. There, according to Armistead Long, "he enjoyed a fine field for exercising his high social qualities and fondness for military display."[13] Magruder's "princely hospitality and brilliant show-drills" achieved him little reward. Plagued by his heavy drinking, his army career seemed destined to go nowhere.

These persistent rumors of Magruder's intemperance made President Jefferson Davis question his ability to maintain command on the Peninsula. Davis instructed Robert E. Lee to ask Magruder about his insobriety. Magruder replied that "the reports of the nature alluded to by you do one great injustice." Prince John concluded that "I will never during this war give the slightest cause for these reports." Lee responded three days later to him that he had spoken to the Confederate president and relayed Magruder's pledge "to abstain altogether from the use of intoxicating drink."[14] His promotion to brigadier general was confirmed, and on 7 October 1861, Magruder was promoted major general.

Major General John Bankhead Magruder, CSA. *Courtesy of Lee Hall Mansion.*

2

Sacrifice

Magruder did not rest on his Big Bethel laurels and continued to strengthen his forward positions as more reinforcements arrived from Richmond. Since Big Bethel and additional fortifications at Howard's Bridge guarded the Hampton-York Road, Magruder also needed to block any advance up the Hampton Road. Also known as the Great Warwick Road, the Hampton Road was the main land transportation link between Hampton and Williamsburg. This road left Hampton, swung across the Peninsula into Warwick County and moved through the county until it crossed Skiffes Creek. There the road continued through James City County into Williamsburg. This same roadway then took travelers on to Richmond. Just below Williamsburg, the road joined with the Yorktown Road. This road connected Williamsburg with Yorktown and was a continuation of the Hampton-York Road.

As the Hampton Road went through Warwick County, it crossed several creeks and rivers, all of which offered excellent defensive opportunities. Any Union movement from Camp Butler toward Williamsburg would use this roadway as an avenue of approach. Accordingly, Magruder established a forward position at Young's Mill on Deep Creek. A "Spy Battalion" under Major John Baytop Cary was organized utilizing three cavalry companies and the Wythe Rifles, whose members were to "act as voitgeurs."[1] Cary's command was sent to Young's Mill to harass Union troop movements. Benjamin Butler was concerned about the Confederate troop movements and intentions. He continued to send his troops to probe the surrounding countryside as a show of force. The Union general believed that he was outnumbered by Magruder's force and continued to call for reinforcements. Butler wrote General Scott:

> *It is among the possibilities and perhaps the probabilities that a concentration of troops may be made at Yorktown via James River, and an advance movement upon this post ensue....Newport News, perhaps can hold out with the three thousand men there against that attack of five thousand or six thousand men, but we have not, as yet, any field artillery here. To defend ourselves outside the fort, we have but about three thousand effective men and some of them not the best troops... The enemy are apparently preparing for an advance movement from Yorktown and the Norfolk troops, should they attack I should be, to say the least, largely outnumbered.*[2]

The chess match on the Peninsula witnessed Butler striving to expand his control beyond Newmarket Creek as Magruder endeavored to limit Union movements up the Peninsula. A Confederate picket was killed on 15 June, and nervous Southerners wounded one of their own cavalry videttes on 16 June. Butler sent two expeditions out from Fort Monroe on 24 June to disrupt Confederate activities. The first was merely a feint toward Big Bethel, with orders not to bring on an engagement. The other had a more meaningful purpose. Elements of the 10th New York marched from Fort Monroe to the mouth of the Back River, where they met the steamers *Adriatic* and *Fanny*, a steam launch from the USS *Roanoke* and several bateaux. The New Yorkers were then ferried upstream with a mission to destroy all vessels involved in trade with the Eastern Shore. The expedition destroyed twelve sailing vessels and several small boats found up the Back River and Harris Creek. The Confederates were powerless to stop this destructive work.

On 28 June, Magruder resolved to strike back when he learned of rumors of a Union advance toward Warwick Court House. The Confederate general left Yorktown with three regiments, artillery and cavalry with the intention of attacking Camp Butler. Magruder's strike force reached the Federal pickets and then fell back to Young's Mill. The next day, Magruder returned to Yorktown. However, he reinforced Young's Mill with the 5th Louisiana and 6th Georgia. These troops continued work on the Young's Mill entrenchments. On 3 July, Magruder learned that a Federal foraging force planned to march up the Warwick (Hampton)

Lieutenant Colonel Charles Didier Dreux, CSA. *Courtesy of the Confederate Memorial Museum.*

Road toward Young's Mill. He ordered Lieutenant Colonel Charles D. Dreux to take the 5th Louisiana, with elements of the Wythe Rifles and artillery, to ambush the Federal foragers. To ensure that he understood the landscape to plan his trap, Magruder's aide-de-camp, Lieutenant Hugh Stanard, advised Dreux "to consult Captain Curtis and his officers, they being acquainted with the country."[3] When Dreux's command surprised elements of the Hawkins's Zouaves near Captain Smith's home, the Confederates were repulsed. Dreux was the first Louisianan and Confederate field-grade officer to be killed during the war. The Confederates immediately sought revenge against the "Lincolnites" as "Colonel Drue's [*sic*] death was mourned by who knew him—on account of his bravery and high military genius,"[4] remembered Lieutenant William J. Stores. Dreux had just written a letter home to his wife with a premonition of his death:

> *We are ordered from this place* [Richmond] *to Yorktown, within eight miles of the enemy's line, and most glorious prospects of an early end and good brush. When there we shall be under the command of Col. Magruder, who succeeded so well in his debut at Bethel Church. The boys are delighted with the prospects before them, and we are all in the highest glee. May the God of Battles smile upon us. Cheer up, my dear wife. I have the brave hearts and strong arms to sustain and cheer me on, and I feel confident of the result. Many a noble son may fall by my side, and I may be the first one to bite the dust, but rest assured that they or I will always be worthy of the esteem and respect of our countrymen, and endeavor to deserve well of our country.*[5]

Major John Bell Hood was able to retaliate on 12 July near the very site of Dreux's death when his cavalry sprung a trap on a two-hundred-member detachment of the Hawkins's Zouaves. The Zouaves were routed with four killed and ten captured. Hood later noted how the Zouaves were defeated with "a great consternation and the enemy ran in all directions through the woods."[6] Magruder called the skirmish "a brilliant little affair…Too much

Captain Francis Lightfoot Lee, CSA.
Courtesy of the Virginia War Museum.

praise," Magruder added, "cannot be bestowed on Major Hood and the cavalry generally for untiring industry in efforts to meet the enemy, and for their energy with which they have discharged their harassing and unusually laborious duties."[7] Despite this defeat, the Federals continued to press beyond Newmarket Creek. Additional skirmishes occurred on 19 and 22 July as both North and South alike strove to control no-man's-land.

Butler was concerned about his communications between Fort Monroe and Camp Butler. Although two steamers operated between the fort and Newport News Point on a daily basis, Butler wanted a more immediate connection. He organized a signal corps under Major Albert J. Myer as chief signal officer. Myer used civilian contractors to operate a telegraph line to link the two fortifications. Richard O'Brien was superintendent of the line, and he was assisted by his younger brother, John, at Fort Monroe, as well as by Jesse Bunnell and Henry Smith at Hampton and by John Lock and John Stough at Camp Butler. This telegraphic line would need constant maintenance as Confederate patrols from Big Bethel would often cut it. Several times John O'Brien was almost captured or shot by a Confederate cavalry patrol. On one occasion, he was out with a mule-drawn wagon, a lineman and some contrabands when he saw an approaching patrol. O'Brien ran into the woods to hide. When the cavalry surrounded the wagon, the teamster waved to O'Brien. He came out of hiding to discover that the patrol was from the 1st New York Mounted Rifles.

Butler was also anxious about his precise knowledge, or lack thereof, of the actual whereabouts of the Confederate positions surrounding the Union enclave on the Peninsula. The Union general arranged for the famous balloonist John La Mountain to come to the Peninsula to serve as the Union's aerial observer. The aeronaut arrived at Fort Monroe

Camp Butler's water battery at Newport News Point, Virginia. *Courtesy of John Moran Quarstein.*

on 25 July. Due to high winds, La Mountain was unable to make a successful flight until 31 July, when he reached a height of 1,400 feet. At that height, he was able to observe a radius of over thirty miles. His next ascension, on 1 August, enabled him to see the Confederate camp at Young's Mill and note that this position held between four thousand and five thousand men. He also reported that the Confederates had an advanced position at Water's Creek on the Warwick Road, as well as the fortifications on Sewell's Point and Pig Point. On 3 August, La Mountain lifted his balloon from the deck of the USS *Fanny* using a windlass and mooring ropes. The balloon reached a height of 2,000 feet and enabled a thorough inspection of the Confederate positions defending Norfolk. A second flight was made on 10 August from the deck of the tug *Adriatic*. La Mountain had by now used up all of his hydrogen gas-making materials and needed to secure these supplies from elsewhere. Before he departed Fort Monroe, La Mountain proposed to General Butler that he could return with a balloon capable of destroying Norfolk. La Mountain further advised Butler that "[b]allooning can be made a very useful implement in warfare."[8]

La Mountain's balloon may have presented an expression of the Union's technological advantage, but it did little to stem the expansion of Confederate strength. The Federal defeat during the Battle of Manassas on 21 July 1861 had repercussions that reached all the way down to the Peninsula. General Scott ordered Butler to send troops to Washington on 24 July. Butler complied immediately and on 27 July sent northward the 3rd, 4th and 5th New York regiments and Colonel Edward Baker's California Regiment to the Union capital. General Butler became very apprehensive about the Union's precarious position on the Peninsula. His command was not only reduced by the units sent to Washington but also by the end of the term of enlistment of ninety-day volunteer units, such as the 2nd and 3rd Massachusetts and the 1st Vermont. He knew that this would open the door to aggressive Confederate actions. He traveled to Washington to meet with Winfield Scott. Butler advised Scott that additional reinforcements were required to maintain control of the Peninsula's tip. He also expressed the need for a more experienced officer to take command of the Union Department of Virginia.

Before Butler went to Washington, he had ordered the evacuation of Hampton. Union troops had occupied the town on 1 July, and during their withdrawal on 25 July, a third of the town was burned. Federal pickets were also removed from Newmarket Creek Bridge and repositioned on the Camp Hamilton side of Hampton Creek.

When the Federals abandoned Hampton, Magruder was prompted to take advantage of this Union retrenchment. He organized a strike force of 1,600 men with cavalry and two artillery batteries. Colonel Robert Johnson, an 1850 West Point graduate, was placed in command of Magruder's mounted troops with the grand title of "Commander-in-Chief of Cavalry, Army of the Peninsula." He was ordered to move toward Newmarket Creek Bridge to sever Union communications between Fort Monroe and Camp Butler and to suppress any Federal troop activity outside their fortifications. His second duty was to sweep through the Lower Peninsula from the Back River to Harwood's Mill to Newport News Point to capture escaping slaves. More than 150 African Americans were apprehended by Confederate troops and then transported to Williamsburg to work on fortifications.

Johnson's raid had provided Magruder with the knowledge that the Federals had removed all but one regiment from Newport News Point. Therefore, on 28 July, the Confederate commander sent a flag of truce to Camp Butler demanding that the Federals abandon their position or be assaulted. Although Magruder recognized that the Union fortifications were too strong for an attack or investment, he continued to demonstrate in front of Camp Butler hoping to draw the Federals into battle. While a small engagement was fought near Salter's Creek, Magruder's attention soon shifted to Hampton.

On 6 August, Magruder, with a force of four thousand infantry, four hundred cavalry and the Richmond Howitzers, marched to within a mile and a half of Newport News Point. Magruder cut the Federal communications and then marched to within a mile of Hampton. During the march toward Hampton, Magruder obtained a copy of the *New York Tribune* from an abandoned Union picket post. Within its pages he learned that Butler intended to reoccupy Hampton as "he did not know what to do with the many negroes in his possession unless he possessed Hampton; they were still coming in rapidly; that as their masters had deserted their homes and slaves, he would consider the latter free, and would colonize them at Hampton, the home of most of their owners."[9] Magruder immediately decided to destroy the town, advising Richmond:

The burning of Hampton, Virginia. *Courtesy of the Virginia War Museum.*

Having known for some time past that Hampton was the harbor of runaway slaves and traitors, and being under the guns of Fort Monroe, it could not be held by us, even if taken, I was decidedly under the impression that it should have been done before, and when I found from the above report of its extreme importance to the enemy, and that the town itself would lend great strength to whatever fortifications they might erect around it, I determined to burn it.[10]

With an agreement from the local soldiers in his command as to the "propriety of this course," and seeing that Butler had already destroyed a third of Hampton when his troops had evacuated the town, Magruder organized a force under the command of Captain Jefferson Curle Phillips of the Old Dominion Dragoons to complete this "loathsome yet patriotic act" prompted by "the foulest desecrations of these houses and homes of our Virginia people by their former Yankee occupants."[11]

Captain Phillips gathered a force of about five hundred men, including the Old Dominion Dragoons, the Mecklenburg Cavalry, the Warwick Beauregards and the York Rangers to destroy the town. Several of these

Captain Jefferson Curle Phillips, Old Dominion Dragoons, CSA, 1861. *Courtesy of the Hampton History Museum.*

soldiers owned property in Hampton. Phillips's command, accompanied by Colonel James G. Hodges's 14th Virginia Infantry, marched across Newmarket Creek Bridge toward Hampton. Once this force reached the brick wall surrounding St. John's Church, the Federal pickets guarding the Hampton Creek Bridge were forced to retreat. As Colonel Hodges's regiment defended the bridge, Phillips sent men through the town to warn the remaining residents of the impending doom. As darkness began to shroud the town, he and his men began their destructive task. Sergeant Robert Hudgins of the Old Dominion Dragoons recounted the scene:

Captain William Stores, 32nd Virginia Infantry Regiment, CSA, 1862. *Courtesy of Leslie Jensen.*

As the smoke ascended toward the heavens I was reminded of the ancient sacrifices on the altar to many deities, and I thought of now my little hometown was being made a sacrifice to the grim god of war.

We raced back to the town to be in at the finish and to participate in the actual work of destruction ere it was too late. By the time we had reached the corner of King and Court streets the Baptist Church was burning like an inferno—the flames belching out of the steeple like a furnace. The courthouse on the opposite was also in flames though it had not been consumed to the extent as had the church. At the cross streets it seemed as if hell itself had broken loose, and as if all of its fiery demons were pouring fuel upon the flames. The light of the flames in the sky gave nearly the luster as if it was midday.

…As we filed out of the town, there rested in the hearts of each of us the realization of a great sacrifice nobly made, and the heroic satisfaction of a soldier's duty well performed. [12]

Lieutenant William J. Stores of the York Rangers sadly wrote in his diary that Hampton's destruction was "patriotism as a principal of action." [13]

3

Prince John's Peninsula

The Federals were shocked by Hampton's destruction. One Northern newspaper called it "a wanton act of cruelty to the resident Unionists, and moreover useless."[1] "Such a picture of war and desolation I never saw nor thought of, and hope I shall not again," wrote Lieutenant Charles Harvey Brewster. "I pass through the churchyard round the celebrated Hampton Church, the oldest one in use in the United States, it is completely destroyed all but the walls and they are useless."[2] Ben Butler could not understand the Confederate scorched earth policy, writing to Winfield Scott, "A more wanton and unnecessary act than the burning, as it seems to me, could not have been committed. I confess myself so poor a soldier as not to be able to discern the strategic importance of this movement."[3] It was an eerie scene.

Hampton's burning was the last major offensive move in the 1861 chess match between the Federals and Confederates on the Peninsula. Both North and South alike recognized the need to consolidate their positions in preparation for the 1862 campaign season. The opposing forces were within view of each other as they sought more men, artillery and supplies to enhance their fortifications.

Ben Butler's request to be relieved of command of the Union Department of Virginia was finally fulfilled on 17 August 1861, when Major General John Ellis Wool arrived as his replacement. Butler left Hampton Roads on 26 August with Flag Officer Silas Horton Stringham's seven-vessel fleet, en route to capturing Hatteras Inlet. The seventy-seven-year-old Wool had served in the U.S. Army for almost fifty years. He assumed his command at

Fort Monroe with the same vigorous leadership that had earned him honors at Queenstown Heights and Plattsburg during the War of 1812. This service elevated Wool to the rank of colonel, and he served as the army's Inspector General from 1816 until his promotion to brigadier general in 1841. He achieved perhaps his greatest fame during the Mexican War when he had rapidly marched his troops nine hundred miles from San Antonio to reinforce Zachary Taylor at the Battle of Buena Vista. Wool was brevetted major general and received the thanks of Congress "for gallant and distinguished conduct" during this action.[4] In early 1861, he commanded the Department of the East until transferred to Virginia by General Scott.

Upon his arrival at Old Point Comfort, Wool continued to improve the Union toehold on the Lower Peninsula. He advocated strengthening Fort Monroe and Camp Butler to threaten Richmond and Norfolk, as well as other points along the Confederate coastline. Wool advised Winfield Scott that

> [t]o operate on this coast with success…we want more troops…If I had 20,000 or 25,000 men, in conjunction with the Navy, we could do much on this coast to bring back from Virginia the troops of North Carolina, South Carolina, and Georgia; but the arrangements should be left to Commodore Stringham and myself. We know better than anyone at Washington attached to the Navy what we require for such expeditions.[5]

Wool recognized that Fort Monroe's command of Hampton Roads not only limited Confederate riverine communications between Norfolk and Richmond and blocked these ports' access to the sea but also, more importantly, provided a valuable springboard for Federal expeditions against other Southern ports.

Fort Monroe's existence as the only Union strategic fortified position in the upper South began to reap dividends by late 1861. The Butler-Stringham Expedition was successful in capturing Hatteras Inlet on 29 August 1861. Stringham, who had served in the U.S. Navy since 1809, was the first commander of the North Atlantic Blockading Squadron. Even though Butler took most of the credit for the operation, it was Stringham's tactics that ensured success. With the loss of only one man killed (caused by Union naval gunnery), Butler's 319-man landing party was able to capture Forts Hatteras and Clark, as well as 670 Confederates and thirty-five cannons. This victory was made possible by Stringham's squadron. Flag Officer Stringham placed his seven steamships in a circle and, while moving, bombarded the Confederate forts. This innovative deployment meant that Stringham's warships were more difficult targets than the stationary coastal forts.

The capture of Hatteras Inlet boosted Butler's reputation as a strategist and, more importantly, proved the value of Fort Monroe for combined operations. Using the Hatteras Inlet operation as a model, the Union used Hampton Roads as a platform for the next three major actions against the Confederate coastline. The next major operation was the DuPont-Sherman Expedition that captured Port Royal Sound, South Carolina. Flag Officer Samuel Francis DuPont, commander of the newly created South Atlantic Blockading Squadron, used Stringham's tactics to subdue Forts Walker and Beauregard, the two forts guarding the entrance to the Pamlico Sound. DuPont's seventeen warships forced the forts to surrender on 7 November 1861. The flag officer then debarked Brigadier General Thomas W. Sherman's 12,000 troops as they occupied South Carolina's barrier islands. Other expeditions quickly followed, including the Burnside-Goldsborough Roanoke Island Expedition and the Farragut-Butler New Orleans Expedition.

Wool still needed more men, as he wrote Winfield Scott on 6 October 1861 that he wanted additional regiments, noting, "I only ask that you will give me sufficient number of troops to defend this place. The enemy have been re-enforcing their troops."[6] Confederate pressure had indeed been increasing all across the no-man's-land between the Confederate positions at Young's Mill and Big Bethel, as well as the Union positions at Camp Butler and Fort Monroe. On 12 October, twelve Federals were captured near Camp Butler. One Southern attempt to ambush a Federal foraging party near Newmarket Creek Bridge only resulted in the Confederates shooting at one another. Additional skirmishes occurred on 11 and 12 November, contesting control of this bridge. By the onset of winter, there was little to forage for in the no-man's-land as both sides had left behind a path of destruction. Farms had been pillaged and barns burned; the lush countryside had become a desolate scene.

Even though many Confederate soldiers shared William Corson's disappointment that "the Yankees never come out from their camp far enough to give us the benefit of a little brush,"[7] Magruder was quite content to concentrate on constructing his fortifications. Although his Army of the Peninsula had grown to almost 9,500 men, thereby outnumbering the Federal force on the Peninsula, the Confederate general constantly feared that the Federals would march against his incomplete defenses. Each troop ship or amphibious force that came into Hampton Roads gave reason for alarm.

Since he had arrived at Yorktown, Magruder focused on expanding and enhancing his defensive system. As soon as the 1st North Carolina arrived in Yorktown in early June 1861, the men were put to work rebuilding Cornwallis's 1781 earthworks. Consequently, Magruder constantly entreated Richmond with requests for more troops, artillery and slaves to work on the three lines of earthworks he wished to build across the Peninsula. His forward line of defense began at Young's Mill on Deep Creek (a tributary of the James River), crossed the Peninsula to Harwood's Mill and Howard's Bridge on the Poquoson River and followed that river to where it emptied into the Chesapeake Bay at Ship's Point. Forward of Young's Mill were some earthworks at Langhorne's Mill on Water's Creek, and Big Bethel, a few miles south of Howard's Bridge, was further fortified. Big Bethel was a staging area for patrols seeking to disrupt Union activities between the two branches of the Back River.

Magruder's second line began at Mulberry Island on the James River and followed the Warwick River to within one and a half miles of Yorktown. This colonial port town was fortified with a series of redoubts, some of them built atop the British works remaining from the 1781 siege. This line was complemented by fortifications on the east side of the York River (which was less than half a mile wide at this point) at Gloucester Point and across the James River to Fort Boykin on Burwell's Bay and Fort Huger on Hardin's Bluff directly across the river from Mulberry Island Point. Both Fort Boykin and the Gloucester Point earthworks dated to the seventeenth century. Parts of the Yorktown fortifications were built atop those constructed by Cornwallis.

Magruder's final defensive position on the Peninsula was developed a few miles below Williamsburg. This position was first proposed by Benjamin S. Ewell; however, it was modified by Captain Alfred Rives into a series of fourteen redoubts, complete with supporting redans and rifle pits, between College and Queen's Creeks. The center of this line was anchored by Fort Magruder (Redoubt #6) astride the Hampton-Williamsburg-Yorktown Road joined together.

Magruder decided to make the Warwick-Yorktown Line his primary Peninsula defensive position. Officers under his command generally concurred with this decision. Colonel Hill Carter, concerned about his loss of artillery for use on Mulberry Island, wrote from Jamestown, "I can only hope that Yorktown and Mulberry Island will be made impregnable, else

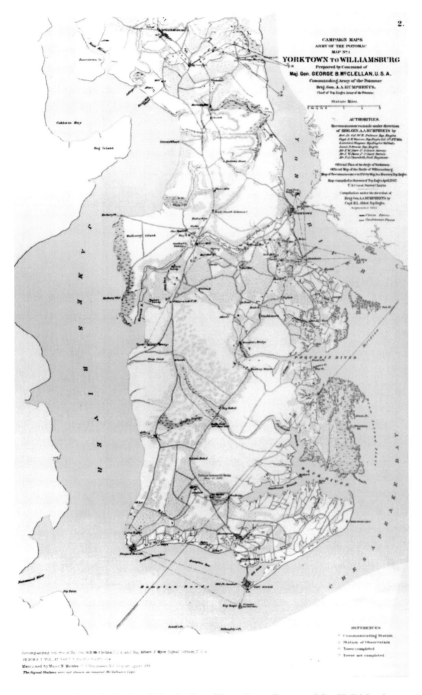

Map of the Virginia Peninsula by Andrew Humphrey. *Courtesy of Lee Hall Mansion.*

Above, left: Colonel Isaac St. John, Chief Engineer, Army of the Peninsula, CSA. *Courtesy U.S. Army Military Historical Institute.*

Above, right: Brigadier General Gabriel Rains, CSA. *Courtesy of U.S. Army Military Historical Institute.*

the Peninsula will be in danger, and perhaps Virginia overrun."[8] Magruder applied all of his furious and apparently inexhaustible energy into building his fortifications. He mobilized every resource available, including as many as six hundred slaves per day and soldiers from his command, to vigorously construct these earthworks. Men were detached to build gun carriages for 32-pounder Columbiads at Macy's Sawmill on the Warwick River, and soldiers who were prewar overseers, such as James P. Hopkins of the 32nd Virginia Infantry, were "detailed to superintend the working on the batteries along the Warwick River."[9] As his troop strength increased, Magruder divided his army into two divisions. Brigadier General Lafayette McLaws commanded the division based at Young's Mill, and Brigadier General Gabriel James Rains was in command of the troops at Yorktown. Rains, an 1827 West Point graduate, was also a veteran of the Mexican and Seminole Wars.

The Confederate command immediately recognized that the Peninsula's James River flank was extremely vulnerable. Unless they were able to close the river to any Federal fleet advance, Union gunboats could simply steam upriver. Magruder noted this problem and advised Richmond on 9 July 1861 that

> [t]*he work contemplated on Mulberry Island, if that point is geographically situated as represented, could be of greatest importance in defending this place and Richmond. If the enemy was forced by such a work to march up the Peninsula, there are several lines which would at once be fortified where he would meet with very rough treatment or be repulsed. I think he would be entirely defeated. At present, and without this work, these lines can easily be turned and landing made above them on James River. If it be decided to fortify at Mulberry Island, no time should be lost.*[10]

Robert E. Lee, then military adviser to President Jefferson Davis, appointed naval officer Captain George N. Hollins to command the James River defenses and advised Magruder that "the construction of the battery at Day's Point and the projected batteries at Mulberry Point, and the one opposite will…diminish the danger of an attempt upon Williamsburg."[11]

Magruder was not quite satisfied, as he was concerned that any water battery on Mulberry Island could not defend the position against a land attack made possible by an amphibious assault. He advised Richmond:

> *Whilst I was extremely glad to hear that works are to be erected on Mulberry Island and opposite, as they will be obstacles to the enemy in any attempt to ascend the river, yet that any work erected on this side of the river could be carried by the enemy, either by storm or by siege on the land side, and then that their ships could pass up. Mulberry Island (so-called) is not an island, but a peninsula, and therefore any work on it, however strong, can be taken…The work at Mulberry Island is very important and ought at once to be built…The spot where the work is to be erected—and that is the proper spot—is cut off from the mainland by an impassable march, but this march is very near where the work is to be, and the ground on the land side of the march commands the work. From this side at a distance of half a mile the enemy could erect batteries of heavy guns and perhaps make our work untenable; at all events much time would be required to make it secure against a land attack.*[12]

On 14 August 1861, work commenced on the Mulberry Island Point water battery under the direction of naval officers. Designed for six cannons,

Fort Crafford, Mulberry Island Point. *Courtesy of the Virginia War Museum.*

the battery mounted only four, and Magruder continued to fear that it would be flanked "if the enemy can land at the mouth of the Warwick River."[13]

The Confederate navy responded. On 26 August, Lieutenant Catesby ap Roger Jones was ordered to sink six canalboats filled with granite and sand in the Swash Channel off Mulberry Island. Magruder wanted more done to block the channels and requested that barges also be sunk at the entrance to the Warwick River.

When Flag Officer Silas Stringham's squadron assembled in Hampton Roads in preparation for his assault on Hatteras Inlet, this large naval force alarmed Magruder and prompted him to alert his troops to an impending Union attack up the James River. He ordered the 14th Virginia to march to Land's End at the southern tip of Mulberry Island and erect fortifications that would command the entrance to the Warwick River. Magruder exhorted the men to "defend your position to the utmost" and added, "also report whether you have sufficient spades to make the work."[14]

Additional reports of Union gunboats operating off Newport News Point made Magruder believe that the Federals had "the intention of going up the James River." Magruder, unsure of the enemy's purpose, advised Colonel James Hodges of the 14th Virginia to "immediately take position with his whole force near the work at Mulberry Island, near Crawford's House, to defend it and prevent a landing so far as may be in your power."[15] A cavalry picket was left at Land's End to watch for any enemy attempt to steam up the Warwick River. Reinforcements from Jamestown, Major J.M. Patton's command containing the Greensville Guards and the Charles City Southern Guards, were also added to the covering force on Mulberry Island.

Although the anticipated Union attack never materialized, Magruder continued to be concerned about his James River flank, believing that everything "must be got and kept in perfect readiness at Mulberry Island." The Confederate general lamented that the defenses that had been erected were plagued by a lack of troops and artillery. President Davis and Adjutant and Inspector General Samuel Cooper often turned a blind eye to Magruder's constant requests. Magruder was chided for calling out the militia to supplement his troop strength, as well as for his impressment of slaves to build his fortifications. He pestered Richmond with requests for support, noting that the newly constructed water batteries on Mulberry Island would be "of no avail unless the embankments which I have caused to be thrown up on the shores there can be furnished with heavy guns."[16] Two 42-pounder carronades were eventually provided for the Land's End battery, and the Confederate navy agreed to station the CSS *Patrick Henry* off Mulberry Island to assist in the defense. A telegraph line was installed, connecting Mulberry Island Point with Lee Hall, Yorktown and Williamsburg to keep Magruder in touch with his weak right flank.

Magruder, despite the approach of the winter season, kept units on alert, moving troops from one position to another to counter Union troop dispositions. The CS Navy finally fulfilled Magruder's request and, on 17 October, sunk rock- and sand-filled canalboats at the mouth of the Warwick River to block its entrance. Magruder was still disheartened by his exposed flank and pressed Richmond for more heavy artillery, writing:

> *It is a matter of great moment that the defenses at…Mulberry Point should be as strong as possible. The work at Mulberry Point can contain two more guns…The river is better commanded at that point than at any other below Jamestown; and if it can be rendered safe there, troops as well as field guns could be used below.*[17]

Magruder even sought to obtain cannons from the Confederate navy:

> *The lowest fort on James River, on the left bank, is Mulberry Island Point; opposite is Harden's Bluff fort, both strong on the water fronts. By a glance at the map it will be seen that if the enemy can land at the mouth of Warwick River, he can march to Mulberry Island Point and take the fort there in the rear. The troops on my line from the mouth of Deep Creek, which is the same as that of Warwick River, cannot go to the succor of Mulberry Island Point without making a march of some 20 miles around the head of Warwick River; besides, the right flank of my own line is below Warwick River. That flank must be secured and the fort at Mulberry*

Island Point, both in full sight of the enemy at Newport News, now at least 8,000 strong. I have therefore caused one regiment (500 strong) to take post at Land's End, on the right, at the mouth of Warwick River, and have thrown up an entrenchment there, but these guns of the Teaser *are necessary for the armament of this entrenchment. I have caused rifle-pits to be made to protect the men, and sunk canal boats across the mouth of the river.* [18]

The Confederate commander's fears only increased when a hurricane devastated the sea level Mulberry Island Point battery later in October. Magruder lamented this calamity, reporting:

The work is in sight of the enemy. Negroes have deserted from it and informed the enemy of the situation. They will attack it, I presume, as soon as they can make preparations, and, if they carry it, as they probably will, in its present state, a great disaster may happen. [19]

The CSS *Patrick Henry* and the CSS *Jamestown* were assigned to guard the James River off Mulberry Island Point to block any further Union advance while work began anew on the fortifications. Besides the skirmishes, constant alerts, various details and earthwork construction, the Confederates serving on the Peninsula spent a comfortable time awaiting the 1862 campaign season. Magruder developed an excellent supply system, as was confirmed by William Corson of Company G, Cumberland Light Dragoons, 3rd Virginia Cavalry, in a letter to his future wife:

Our camp teams with market wagons every morning that bring vegetables, butter, eggs, chickens, shoats, watermelons and most anything that can be had at the Richmond market. There is the finest crop of sweet potatoes raised here that I ever saw grow anywhere. Our boys have feasted on fine fish and watermelons until it is difficult to find sale for them…Oystering will soon commence and then we will feast indeed. Taking all things into consideration, I think this is the most delightful country I ever saw and but for the chills, I would rather live here than any place I know. The streams here furnish the finest fish in the world and team with waterfowl in the fall and winter. The growing crop of corn, where it is worked, is excellent and if it can be saved, will feed the army here a long time. [20]

The Peninsula appeared to these soldiers as a land of plenty. Oyster-eating contests were extremely popular. A friendly competition ensued to prove whether or not the Warwick River variety was more succulent than those from the York River.

All was not perfect, though, as many soldiers complained of nights when "musketeers [mosquitoes] swarmed around in myriads." Sickness of all types affected the soldiers greatly. The first recorded death for the Warwick Beauregards (Company H, 32nd Virginia Infantry) was Private William R. Smith, who succumbed to typhoid fever on 24 July 1861. Another soldier lamented that the only thing that they had in abundance "other than rain and mud was sickness."[21] The 15th North Carolina Infantry Regiment, numbering almost 1,100 officers and soldiers, was ordered to the Army of the Peninsula in late July 1861. The regiment was assigned to construct earthworks; however, by August, more than 80 percent of the men were stricken with fever. The entire regiment was reassigned to a healthier location since the men, who were primarily from the Piedmont section of North Carolina, were not used to the Tidewater climate. Almost 15 percent of the 15th North Carolina died from sickness that summer. Sickness was commonplace among the various units unused to the "swelter and pestilential marshes of the Peninsula."[22] About one half of Dreux's Battalion were taken ill in August 1861, and in September, only 100 men of Coppens's Battalion were fit for duty. Brigadier General Lafayette McLaws wrote his wife on 21 July 1861 that he visited the General Hospital in Williamsburg and noted "there are about one hundred patients with measles, mumps, and all kinds of diseases such as soldiers have."[23] Fevers and other ailments were rampant; nevertheless, Magruder believed that the "medical officers deserve the highest commendation for the skill and devotion with which they performed their duty in this sickly country."[24]

Despite the diseases that raged though the camps, the Confederates were able to build comfortable winter quarters nestled among their fortifications. William White of the Richmond Howitzers wrote from Mulberry Island:

Private George Washington Smith, Peninsula Artillery. *Courtesy of Kirby Smith.*

We have comfortable cabins, built by our own men, with glass windows, plank floors, kitchen attached, etc....Time does not hang very heavily on my hands, for I am now drilling a company of infantry...Then we get up an occasional game of ball or chess, or an old hare hunt...Fortunately we have managed to scrape up quite a goodly number of books, and being in close communication with Richmond, we hear from our friends daily.[25]

These comforts aside, the soldiers remained constantly aware of the battles that would surely come in the spring, as White noted:

Soon the Spring campaign will open and then farewell to the quiet pleasures of "Rebel Hall."....No more winters during the war will be spent as comfortably and carelessly as this. Soon it will be a struggle for life, and God only knows how it will all end. My health has but little improved, but I had rather die in the army than live out.[26]

Magruder's right was based at Young's Mill, and these troops formed part of Brigadier General Lafayette McLaws's command. The left flank, focused on the defense of Yorktown and Gloucester Point, was manned by Brigadier General Gabriel Rains's division. The Army of the Peninsula was composed of units from Virginia, North Carolina, Florida, Georgia and Louisiana. Local commands helped these units acclimate themselves to the Peninsula.

Several companies raised on the Peninsula were amalgamated into the 32nd Virginia Volunteer Infantry, initially commanded by Colonel Benjamin Stoddert Ewell. One of the companies, the Warwick Beauregards, was organized just as General B.F. Butler began expanding the Union position on the tip of the Peninsula. The unit consisted of men from upper Warwick County and Mulberry Island. They were recruited into service by Humphrey Harwood Curtis of Endview Plantation, a graduate of Jefferson Medical College, who became the company's commander.

Captain Humphrey Harwood Curtis, Warwick Beauregards, 32nd Virginia Infantry Regiment, 1861. *Courtesy of Elizabeth F.S. Bentien.*

Curtis was one of two doctors in Warwick County and had no previous military experience. The Warwick Beauregards was a rural company and typified the image of a deferential Southern society led by plantation owners. The company leaders were all wealthy men, led by 1st Lieutenant William G. Young of Denbigh Plantation. He had more than $33,000 in real estate and personal property worth $85,000, including his 137 slaves. "Timber Getter" Virginius Nash followed in wealth with a net value of $39,000. The Curtis family dominated the roster, with nine family members serving in the company. Captain H.H. Curtis had real estate holdings valued at over $8,000 and personal assets of $21,000. His brother, 2nd Lieutenant Thomas Glanville Harwood Curtis, was worth more than $7,000, and 4th Corporal William H. Curtis was worth $16,000. But not all members of the company claimed the title of landed gentry; most of the sixty-seven privates enlisting held property valued between $100 and $300, with few exceptions. The men of the Beauregards averaged 27.12 years of age, with occupations mainly as farmers, although the roster included three merchants, eleven laborers, one lawyer, one sailor, one coachmaker and one constable. Ralph Copeland, age fourteen, was the drummer boy. The Warwick Beauregards entered Confederate service following a gala at Captain Curtis's Endview Plantation. The men marched to Williamsburg on 27 May 1861; here the company was mustered into Confederate service along with other Peninsula companies such as the Wythe Rifles, Peninsula Artillery and York Rangers.

Perhaps the most unique and flamboyant troops in Magruder's army were the several Louisiana Zouave regiments. The 2nd, 5th, 10th and 14th Louisiana Volunteers, as well as Coppens's and Dreux's Battalions, were assigned to the Peninsula. The 14th Louisiana, commanded by Colonel Valery Sulakowski, was also known as the "Polish Regiment," containing soldiers from throughout Europe. Sulakowski was a Polish noble who immigrated to the United States after the 1848 Hungarian Revolution. He was a strict disciplinarian and one of the few who could control the wild soldiers who typified the Louisiana Zouaves. Entrained to Virginia, Sulakowski had to shoot several of his raucous, drunken men during a stopover in Grand Junction, Tennessee. The Coppens's Zouaves were especially noted for their drunkenness. The *Richmond Dispatch* noted that "their principal fare...has been crackers, cheese and whiskey."[27] Lafayette McLaws noted that the Louisiana Zouaves units had "the reputation of being the most lawless in existence." McLaws added that the 10th Louisiana was "on Jamestown Island for twelve hours & during that time, tis said, eat up everything on the island, but the horses, and their own species." He also told his wife the story that "the Zouave who had been watching a pig for some time, waiting for him to come into his vicinity, lying flat on the ground for the double purpose of concealing himself from the pig & from general observation, when a North Carolinian coming along boldly shot the pig. The Zouave immediately rose up on his hands and shouted out, 'Aha, de Zouave is not the only one who shoots de pig, some body else is the d___d rascal besides.'" A few found justification in their foraging, as Benjamin Smith of the 5th Louisiana wrote:

Brigadier General Lafayette McLaws, CSA. *Courtesy of Museum of the Confederacy.*

> *I loaded my musket once or twice with the expectation of hurting someone, but was disappointed....As for my bayonet it had only been stained by the blood of an unfortunate pig, who was foolish enough to tempt a hungry soldier. I devoutly hope, that, he was a Yankee pig.*[28]

Despite the alerts and brief skirmishes, the Army of the Peninsula soldiers often complained that their lives were "Dull, dull, dull,"[29] as William E. Monroe of Dreux's Battalion expressed. Leon Jastreminski of the 10th Louisiana recalled a typical day when he wrote to a friend:

> *Reveille at 5 o'clock a.m. Roll call. Then we cook our breakfast which of course we are supposed to eat. Half past eight, guard mounting, which is equal to a small parade....At 9 o'clock company drill until 10 o'clock, after which we are free until 12 o'clock when we have dinner call, and which comes what is called fatigue duty which means spades and _____ and when there is no digging to be done, we have to clean up Quarters. After which we are again free until 6 o'clock. Then dress parade & dismiss [to] cook our supper, eat, loaf & spin yarns until 9 o'clock when Tattoo beats & all are sent to bed like a parcel of school boys.... This occurring every day makes it very tiresome.*[30]

Even though Magruder employed hundreds of slaves per day constructing earthworks, his troops also labored extensively on his system of fortifications. Troops complained that the work with picks, axes and spades was more plentiful than anything else. Lafayette McLaws wrote often to his wife about the work of his soldiers building dams, obstructions and earthworks. He noted that he could not finish his letter as he had to "go off about a mile to put a working party with axes cutting down a grove of fruit trees that obstructed the field of fire of one of the batteries, and to entangle a ravine that led up to within a few hundred yards of me of the batteries."[31] McLaws seemed pleased with the work of his men as he noted that the "main work here is called Fort Magruder, is fast approaching completion, and on the right and left redoubts of formidable strength are either already finished or will be within a week."[32] Magruder was satisfied with all of this work; however, he recognized that his men did not come to the Peninsula to dig but rather to fight the enemy. The Army of the Peninsula knew that that day would soon arrive.

John Bankhead Magruder was the heart and soul of the Army of the Peninsula. He appeared everywhere, entreating his men to prepare for the enemy's advance. His commanding presence, martial spirit and determination boosted his soldiers' morale. He constantly requested more men, cannons and supplies from Richmond. His call-up of militia, impressment of slaves and endless requisitions for war material did not endear him to the Confederate high command. Furthermore, rumors about his drinking persisted, even though he wrote Lee on 8 August 1861, "I think I shall never use any stimulant as long as I live, as my health is perfect without it and as I consider myself bound in honor to abstain from it during the war."[33] George Wythe Randolph was surprised to learn that "reports very injurious to General Magruder were rife in the community, and that he is currently being very dissipated." Randolph tried to counter these rumors and declared to Assistant Secretary of War Albert T. Bledsoe that Magruder "had not used intoxicating liquors of any sort."[34] While Randolph vouched for the Army of the Peninsula commander, stories about Magruder's drinking were commonplace among his soldiers.

While there is no real evidence that Magruder drank on duty, stories abound about his parties, drinking and womanizing. Magruder had an open affair with the wife of the Army of the Peninsula's acting chief medical officer Dr. C.H. Richardson. Formerly a surgeon with the 6th Georgia Volunteers, Richardson felt damned by his wife's scandalous behavior. Magruder and Mrs. Richardson would flirt and dance into the early morning hours. Dr. Robert Leach of the 2nd North Carolina Battalion recounted one tawdry evening. During a ball, sponsored by Colonel Valery Sulakowski of the 14th Louisiana, "the great Paragon of Virtue and Sobriety Gen. Magruder was

so drunk that he fell from the arm of the whore he was dancing with and would have burned to death had he not been pulled from the fire by one of his orderlies. He and the same wench went down on another frolic last Sunday night."[35] During the 1862 Mardi Gras season, members of Dreux's Battalion played a prank on Magruder during the celebrations. The baby-faced Billy Campbell dressed as a woman and strode into the ball on the arm of Ned Phelps. Phelps introduced Campbell to Magruder as an unmarried sister of one of his fellow soldiers. "The gallant Magruder quickly took the 'lady's' hand and began entertaining Campbell with food, drink, and lively conversation."[36] Meanwhile, several other battalion members went to a bedroom above Magruder and, using a mattress, pushed feathers through the cracks in the floorboards. Magruder was covered with feathers as the men all shouted that it was a "Louisiana snowstorm." Campbell and Phelps slipped away, leaving the general rather confused. While more stories surfaced about Magruder's drinking and D.H. Hill claimed that "Magruder...is always drunk and giving foolish and absurd orders,"[37] there were many, like Colonel Thomas R.R. Cobb of Cobb's Legion, who "denied, emphatically and repeatedly, that Magruder was guilty of drunkeness."[38] Perhaps a reporter from the *San Antonio Light* expressed Magruder's personality best when he wrote:

Magruder was a wonderful man. He stood six feet four inches in height, and had a form that men envied and women adored. His nerves were all iron. Foreign travel and comprehensive culture had given him the zest that was always crisp and sparking...he could fight all day and dance all night.

Sketch of Fort Magruder by Robert Sneden. *Courtesy of the Virginia Historical Society.*

In the morning a glass of brandy and a good cigar renewed his strength and cause the cup of his youth to run over with the precious wine of health and good spirits.[39]

Magruder maintained his Army of the Peninsula in an outstanding fashion, preparing his men and defenses to an eventual Union assault. One of his staff officers, Joseph L. Brent, believed that the general was the perfect person to command the Peninsula. He wrote, "Genl. Magruder was well fitted for the task confided to him. He had the faculty of an engineer in discovering strong and weak localities to be defended, and allowed no detail to escape him in way of preparation." Brent recognized Magruder's brilliance in how the general planned to defend the Peninsula with his in-depth fortifications, as well as by using "many methods of exhibiting an aggressive strength."[40]

Almost six months had now passed since the Battle of Big Bethel. Battle lines had been drawn, but the defenses were still incomplete. The commanders on the Lower Peninsula were both concerned that the enemy could capture their exposed positions and accordingly requested that their governments provide them with more men and armaments. Each used the rationale that his position was critical to the success of the war effort. Magruder and Wool recognized the Peninsula's strategic importance as a springboard for attack and as an avenue of defense. They were both determined to use their minimal resources to secure control of Hampton Roads and the Peninsula. The next six months would witness the eyes of America focused on Hampton Roads.

4

A Plan Emerges

General Magruder had spent the winter of 1861–62 expanding his defenses and feared that the Federals would attack before his work was complete. Great alarm was spread when Burnside assembled his amphibious force destined to attack Roanoke Island, North Carolina. Although this Union force would sail away, Magruder continued to worry about his James River flank. He expanded the Mulberry Island defenses by building a covering work half a mile away from the water battery on high ground. Built around the Crafford farmhouse, it was designed to protect the water battery from land attack. Fort Crafford would become the largest earthwork in the Warwick-Yorktown Line, covering almost eight acres. The pentagon-shaped fort had an eight-foot-high outer wall, a dry moat and an inner wall almost twenty feet high. Armed with eight heavy cannons with emplacements for eight smaller pieces, Magruder called Fort Crafford "very strong" and considered it capable of withstanding a month-long siege.

If there was a glaring weakness, it was the troop strength of the Army of the Peninsula. Magruder's command had been increased to thirteen thousand men, but on 4 March 1862, he was ordered to detach five thousand men to Suffolk. The Confederate government knew that the Federals were planning an offensive in Tidewater Virginia; however, Davis and Lee were unsure exactly where the attack might land. Norfolk appeared to be the likely target, especially since Burnside's campaign had already reached as far as Elizabeth City, North Carolina, near the entrance to the Great Dismal Swamp Canal. With Fort Monroe as a base and the U.S. Navy's ability to control the waterways, the Confederacy's control of southeastern Virginia seemed at risk.

The Union war machine was finally stirring on almost every front in early 1862. The Federal successes in Tennessee and along the Mississippi River had the Confederacy in dire straits. President Lincoln was anxious to deliver the coup de grace. He believed that a blow against Richmond might well win the war. The Army of the Potomac had been poised outside of Washington ready to march since late 1861; however, the army's commander hesitated to order this huge force into action. Lincoln's goal in early 1862 was to prompt Major General George Brinton McClellan to launch a campaign to capture the Confederate capital.

George McClellan had arrived in Washington in August 1861, following the Bull Run debacle. Named the commander of the Army of the Potomac, he quickly set himself reorganizing the army into a well-trained, well-supplied and well-armed fighting force. McClellan had taken a large group of raw volunteers and turned it into a cohesive army. McClellan, just thirty-four years old, was totally confident in his ability to achieve great success. He believed that he had been called on to save the nation.

McClellan was born in Philadelphia, Pennsylvania, on 3 December 1826. The son of a prominent doctor, McClellan attended local preparatory schools and the University of Pennsylvania until 1842, when he entered West Point. He graduated at the age of nineteen, second in his class. McClellan was appointed 2nd lieutenant in the Corps of Engineers and served with Winfield Scott's army during its advance on Mexico City. His gallant service and capability to construct bridges and roads earned him two brevets. Following the Mexican War, he worked on the construction of Fort Delaware and the Red River Expedition's transcontinental railway surveys and as an instructor at West Point. He translated and adapted a French manual on bayonet drill and was a member of a board of officers sent to Europe to study European armies during the Crimean War, resulting in McClellan being a co-author of the Delafield Report. This experience enabled him to develop the "McClellan saddle" (M1858), which remained in use by the U.S. Army until its cavalry units were disbanded in the twentieth century.

McClellan resigned his commission in 1857 and became the chief engineer of the Illinois Central Railroad. In 1860, he moved to Cincinnati, Ohio, as president of the Ohio & Mississippi Railroad. When the Civil War erupted, McClellan was named major general of the Ohio Volunteers by Governor William Dennison. "Little Mac," as McClellan was fondly nicknamed, was then made major general, Regular Army, and given command of the Department of Ohio on 3 May 1861.

When several pro-Union western counties of Virginia seceded from the Commonwealth to rejoin the Union, McClellan organized a force of almost 20,000 men and moved into that mountainous region. A small force of Confederates totaling 4,500 men, commanded by Brigadier General Robert S. Garnett, attempted to block McClellan's advance. On 11 July, McClellan sent Brigadier General William Starke Rosencran's brigade up the slopes of Rich Mountain during a heavy rain. Rich Mountain was captured, and the surviving Confederates fell back in disarray, only to be defeated once again at Carrick's Ford on 13 July 1861. McClellan won instant fame for his troops' victory, which secured western Virginia for the Union, as well as control of the important Baltimore & Ohio Railroad.

Major General George Brinton McClellan, USA. *Courtesy of the Library of Congress.*

George McClellan was one of the first Northern heroes of the war. Following Irvin McDowell's defeat at First Bull Run, McClellan immediately set himself to the task of rebuilding the demoralized army. The Army of the Potomac quickly grew in size and confidence under his guidance. The general, now also known as the "Young Napoleon," became the idol of his men. He could be seen riding through the streets of Washington on his seventeen-hands-high dark bay horse, Daniel "Devil Dan" Webster, rushing from camp to conference to camp at breakneck speed, displaying a dash and soldierly presence that impressed soldier and civilian alike. McClellan was full of confidence and believed that he was "the power of the land."[1] The Young Napoleon reached the apex of military power when, on 1 November 1861, Lincoln named him to replace the aged and infirmed Winfield Scott as general-in-chief of the Federal armies. Lincoln worried that he had perhaps placed too heavy a responsibility on the young soldier's shoulders. McClellan merely replied, "I can do it all."[2]

Pressure, however, was beginning to mount for McClellan to take some action against the nearby Confederate army at Manassas Junction. The Union capital was virtually blockaded by Confederate batteries on the lower Potomac. It was an embarrassment to the Union, and the Radical Republicans howled that McClellan, a Democrat who had made no effort to disguise his politics or his dislike of the antislavery movement, was in league with the secessionists. Lincoln, frustrated by McClellan's continual delays, ordered the Army of the Potomac in January to march against the enemy no later than 22 February 1862. McClellan demurred, stating that he was in the process of finalizing a grand strategic plan to capture Richmond and end the war. Known as the Urbanna Plan, McClellan proposed to move his entire army to Annapolis, Maryland, and then down the Chesapeake Bay to the Rappahannock River. The landing at Urbanna, McClellan explained, would threaten the Confederate lines of supply and communication, as would interposing the Union army between General Joseph E. Johnston's army near Manassas and the Confederate capital. While McClellan put forth that the Urbanna Plan would avoid the costly casualties that would surely come from a direct march through northern Virginia to Richmond, Lincoln and Secretary of War Edwin Stanton were skeptical about the plan, especially since it would leave Washington virtually unprotected. Nonetheless, Lincoln agreed to the concept, provided McClellan would leave forty thousand men to defend the capital. Little Mac reluctantly accepted this condition and began planning his campaign.

Simultaneous with McClellan's presentation of his grand plan to bypass the main Confederate army by way of Urbanna, that army's commander, General Joseph Eggleston Johnston (a close prewar friend of McClellan's), was concerned about his advanced position near Manassas. Johnston had almost forty-five thousand men but feared that his army would either be flanked or overwhelmed by McClellan's much larger force. On 20 February, Johnston met with President Jefferson Davis and advised him that his army must retreat to the Rappahannock River in early spring. Davis, beset by Federal advances at virtually every front, could only accept Johnston's decision.

Davis and Johnston did not have a good relationship. They had known each other since their West Point days; however, they were not friends. Joseph Eggleston Johnston was born at his family's estate, Longwood, in Farmville, Virginia, on 3 February 1807. He graduated from West Point in 1829. He and Robert E. Lee befriended each other there. Johnston was assigned to the artillery branch and served in the Black Hawk and

Seminole Wars until he resigned in 1837 to work as a civil engineer in Florida. When an expedition of which he was a part was attacked by Seminoles and routed, Johnston took command of the rear guard and, despite being wounded twice, conducted the retreat with great skill and courage. Consequently, he was named 1st lieutenant, Topographical Engineers, and brevetted captain. Johnston was a hero during the Mexican War and led the column that captured Chapultepec. He was wounded five times and received three brevets. During the antebellum years, Johnston served as inspector general of Albert Sidney Johnston's Utah Expedition. His U.S. Army career climaxed when Johnston was promoted brigadier general and named quartermaster general.

When Virginia left the Union, Johnston joined the Confederacy. Since he was the highest-ranking officer to leave the old army, he expected to receive the corresponding rank in the Confederate army. His hopes were not fulfilled. Davis named five full generals, and Johnston's date of rank placed him fourth, with Samuel Cooper, Albert Sidney Johnston and Robert E. Lee ahead of him and only P.G.T. Beauregard beneath him. Johnston was incensed and began a feud with President Davis over his ranking. His grievance was never resolved. Nevertheless, Johnston was credited, along with P.G.T. Beauregard, with the victory at First Manassas and retained command of the

Confederate army there. Johnston, who had a jaunty appearance and a somewhat magnetic personality, was surprised to learn when he returned to Manassas following his conference with Davis that news of his impending retreat had already been leaked. He resolved to limit his correspondence with Davis about military secrets and ordered a retreat to the Rappahannock River on 5 March 1862. On 6 March, the batteries on the Potomac were abandoned, and units began leaving their trenches along Bull Run on 7 March. By the evening of 9 March, all the Confederates were gone from Manassas. A great deal of equipment and food, including

General Joseph Eggleston Johnston, CSA. *Courtesy of the National Archives.*

numerous heavy cannons and other much needed war material, was left behind in Johnston's haste to retreat. Johnston was severely criticized for his disorganized retreat. The heavy guns he abandoned were not even spiked. A meatpacking plant at Thoroughfare Gap containing more than 100,000 pounds of meat was burned.

On 7 March, McClellan held a council of his general officers to finalize the Urbanna Plan. He sought a vote of confidence for the concept, and his commanders voted eight to four in favor of the plan. The next day, McClellan and his commanders reviewed his plans with Lincoln. Once again, Lincoln agreed to the concept, provided that the Confederate batteries on the Potomac be captured, sufficient troops left behind to defend Washington and the campaign initiated in ten days. McClellan accepted all of these conditions; however, events were already unfolding at Manassas and in Hampton Roads that would completely change the strategic picture.

5

Ironclads

When the Confederates secured Gosport Navy Yard in April 1861, they recognized that it provided them with the opportunity to create an ironclad. Confederate Secretary of the Navy Stephen Russell Mallory realized that the South could not match the North's shipbuilding capacity, so he advised the Confederate Congress that "I regard the possession of an iron-armored ship as a matter of the first necessity. Such a vessel at this time could traverse the entire coast of the United States, prevent all blockades, and encounter, with a fair prospect of success their entire Navy."[1]

To achieve this goal, Mallory approved the conversion of the scuttled steam-screw frigate *Merrimack* into an ironclad. The frigate was raised, placed into dry dock and transformed into a ship the likes of which had never been seen. The 170-foot-long casemate consisted of 24 inches of oak and pine backing, sheathed with two layers of iron plate, 2 inches thick by 6 inches wide. The casemate sides were sloped at a thirty-six-degree angle to deflect shot, but the acute slope only allowed 7 feet of headroom and a beam of 30 feet. The Confederate ironclad was armed with the finest possible heavy cannons. She would carry a broadside battery of six IX-inch Dahlgrens and two 6.4-inch Brooke rifles. Two of the Dahlgren smoothbores were hot-shot guns. A 7-inch Brooke rifle rested on a pivot mount at each end of the casemate, where the structure was pierced by three gun ports. In addition to this armament, a 1,500-pound cast-iron ram was attached to the ironclad's bow.

The Confederates were in a rush to finish their warship; news of the construction of several Union ironclads meant that the South might lose its armored advantage if the vessel was not quickly put into action. The project encountered daily delays, particularly in iron production, but the reconfigured ship finally was launched on 17 February 1862, and commissioned the CSS *Merrimack*. She appeared to be powerful; however, there were numerous defects, including the reuse of the previously condemned engines, a draft too deep (twenty-two feet) and a poorly mounted ram.

Flag Officer Franklin Buchanan was detailed as commander of the James River defenses with the *Virginia* as his flagship. Buchanan, a forty-six-year veteran of the U.S. Navy and the U.S. Naval Academy's first superintendent, was a dynamic officer. "A typical product of the old-time quarter-deck," Lieutenant John Randolph Eggleston, one of the *Virginia*'s officers, wrote of Buchanan. He was "as indomitably courageous as Nelson and as arbitrary."[2] Mallory expected great things of Buchanan and the *Virginia* and wrote the flag officer that "the *Virginia* is a novelty in naval construction, is untried and her power unknown…Her powers as a ram are regarded as formidable, and it is hoped that you may be able to test them. Like a bayonet charge of infantry, this mode of attack, while most distinctive, will commend itself to you in this present scarcity of ammunition." The navy secretary also suggested that the ironclad should make a dashing cruise on "the Potomac as far as Washington, its effect on the public mind would be important to our cause." Such a bold move could bring victory at a time when the Confederacy was reeling from defeats in Tennessee and the Carolina sounds. Mallory was convinced that "the opportunity and means for striking a blow for our Navy are now for the first time presented." The secretary concluded his letter by stating that "[a]ction—prompt and successful action—now would be important for our cause."[3]

Mallory's instructions were not lost on Franklin Buchanan. He selected Newport News Point as his target, but his hopes for a joint army-navy attack were dashed by the unwillingness of Major General John Bankhead Magruder to cooperate. Undaunted, Buchanan still intended to take his ironclad into action as quickly as was feasible. A gale forced him to call off attacks on 6 and 7 March as the *Virginia* needed calm waters in which to operate.

On 8 March, the weather cleared, and Buchanan prepared the *Virginia* for action. Buchanan had his flag officer pendant hoisted, and at 11:00 a.m., the *Virginia* steamed away from the quay. As she made her way down the Elizabeth River, accompanied by her gunboat consorts *Beaufort* and *Raleigh*, both sides of the riverbank were "thronged with people." The *Virginia*'s surgeon, Dinwiddie Phillips, commented that "most of them, perhaps, [were] attracted by our novel appearance, and desirous of witnessing our moments through the water." He added that "[f]ew, if any, entertained an exalted idea of our efficiency, and many predicted a total failure."[4] Meanwhile, the *Virginia*'s crew became aware of many problems with the ship. "From the start we saw that she was slow, not over five knots," Lieutenant John Taylor Wood later commented. "She steered so badly that, with her great length it took thirty to forty minutes to turn…She was as unmanageable as a water-logged vessel."[5]

As the ironclad entered Hampton Roads, the Federal fleet, including five major warships—the sloop *Cumberland* (24 guns) and frigates *Congress* (52 guns), *Minnesota* (47 guns), *Roanoke* (42 guns) and *St. Lawrence* (50 guns), a formidable force of 215 guns—was visible in the distance, arrayed between Newport News Point and Fort Monroe. Undaunted by such force, Buchanan informed his crew, "Sailors in a few minutes you will have the long awaited opportunity to show your devotion to your country and our cause. Remember that you are about to strike for your country and your homes, your wives, and your children. The Confederacy expects everyman to do your duty, beat to quarters."[6] Midshipman Hardin Littlepage recalled Buchanan reminding everyone that "many Confederates had complained that they were taken near enough to the enemy and [he] assured us that there should be no complaint this time, for he intended to head directly for the *Cumberland*." Buchanan concluded his exhortations with the admonition that "[t]hose ships must be taken…Go to your guns."[7]

Even though the Federals knew about the Confederate ironclad project, they were surprised by the *Virginia*'s appearance. As the ship cleared the Elizabeth River, a crewman aboard the *Congress*, anchored near the *Cumberland* off Newport News Point, noted that "I believe that thing is acomin' down at last."[8] To the Union sailors, the *Virginia* looked like "the roof of a very big barn belching forth as from a chimney on fire."[9]

Steaming across Hampton Roads, the ironclad headed for the *Cumberland*. As she passed the *Congress*, the ironclad delivered a devastating broadside of shell and hot shot into the frigate. She then slammed into the *Cumberland*'s starboard quarter, losing her ram in the process but leaving an enormous hole in the sloop's side. Shot and shell from Union warships and shore batteries harmlessly bounced off the *Virginia*'s casemate "like peas from a pop gun" while she exchanged broadsides with the sinking *Cumberland*. The sloop's acting commander, Lieutenant George Upham Morris, gave the

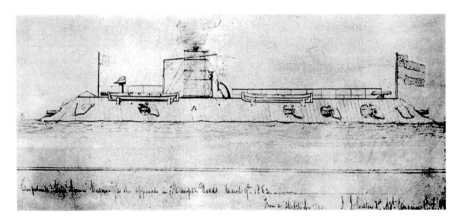

CSS *Virginia. Courtesy of The Mariners' Museum.*

order to abandon ship at 3:35 p.m., exhorting the remaining crew members to "Give 'em a Broadside boys, as She goes!"[10] "She went down bravely, with her colors flying,"[11] remembered Catesby Jones. The *Cumberland's* masts protruded above the waves, the flag marking the spot where 121 Union sailors had gallantly perished.

Having destroyed the *Cumberland*, Buchanan now turned his ironclad toward the USS *Congress*. The *Virginia*, because of her deep draft and poor steering, was forced to go up the James River to complete her turn. As she completed this maneuver, the *Virginia* destroyed two transports and exchanged fire with the shore batteries. The ironclad then steamed within a few hundred yards of the grounded *Congress* and shelled the frigate into submission within thirty minutes. When Buchanan sent the *Raleigh* and *Beaufort* alongside to accept the surrender of the burning frigate, Brigadier General Joseph Fenno King Mansfield, an 1822 West Point graduate, ordered his men to fire on the Confederates. This act enraged Buchanan as he stood atop the *Virginia*, and he began shooting at the Federal soldiers on the shore. He was shot and badly wounded. As he was being taken below, Buchanan ordered Catesby Jones to "Destroy that _____ ship....Plug hot shot into her and don't leave her until she's afire."[12]

Soon the *Congress* was burning from stem to stern. Jones then steered the *Virginia* back into Hampton Roads to attack the three other Union frigates, all of which had run aground. Unfortunately, darkness was coming and the tide receding. He ordered the Confederate ironclad to Sewell's Point for the evening. The *Minnesota* and *St. Lawrence* were hit by several shells, and Jones knew that he would be able to attack them in the morning.

Sinking of the *Cumberland*. *Courtesy of The Mariners' Museum.*

When daylight came on Sunday, 9 March 1862, the *Minnesota*, despite all efforts to float her, was still aground. There appeared nothing that the warship could do but to wait for the *Virginia*'s arrival. The frigate's commander, Captain Gershom Jacques Van Brunt, was prepared to destroy his ship rather than allow it to be captured by the Confederate ironclad.

The *Virginia* got underway from her Sewell's Point mooring at about 6:00 a.m., accompanied by the *Patrick Henry*, *Jamestown* and *Teaser*. Due to a heavy fog, the small fleet delayed entering Hampton Roads until nearly 8:00 a.m. Jones saw the *Minnesota* still stranded on the shoal as the *Virginia* closed within range. Two shells from the Confederate ironclad struck the Union frigate, and the Confederates believed that they would quickly destroy the Federal wooden warship; however, out from the side of the *Minnesota* came, according to Ashton Ramsay, "a barrel-head afloat with a cheesebox on top of it...and boldly confronted us."[13] It was the USS *Monitor*.

The USS *Monitor*'s appearance in Hampton Roads the night before was a virtual miracle. While the *Monitor* was not designed to counter the threat of the Confederate ironclad, it was fortunate that the Union ironclad arrived in time to disrupt the *Virginia*'s destructive work.

She was a completely new concept of naval design, created by Swedish-American inventor John Ericsson. While the *Virginia* was a brilliant adaptation of materials at hand, the *Monitor* was an engineering marvel, containing several patents obtained by Ericsson. The ironclad was 173 feet in length, weighed 776 tons and had a beam of 41.5 feet. Her draft was 11 feet, with a freeboard of less than a foot. The *Monitor* was virtually awash with the sea. All of the ship's machinery, magazine and quarters were positioned below the waterline. The turret and pilothouse were the only features protruding from the deck. The *Monitor*'s most impressive feature was her steam-powered, rotating, circular turret mounting two XI-inch Dahlgren smoothbores. The turret was constructed of eight layers of one-inch-thick, curved, rolled plates. The gun ports were equipped with iron shutters. The turret had an interior diameter of 20 feet and a height of 9 feet. A pilothouse was the only other main feature protruding from the deck. It was a rectangular box of iron, standing 3 feet above the deck and made of nine- by twelve-inch iron bars. A one-inch observation slit was included below the upper tier of iron bars.

Lieutenant John Lorimer Worden was selected as the *Monitor*'s commander. Worden had served in the U.S. Navy since 1834 and had been a prisoner of the Confederates after conducting a secret mission to Fort Pickens in Pensacola Bay, Florida. Recently exchanged, Worden accepted the command of the experimental warship and commented, "After a hasty examination of her [I was] induced to believe that she may prove a success. At all events, I am quite willing to be an agent in testing her capabilities."[14] Not all of her crew were

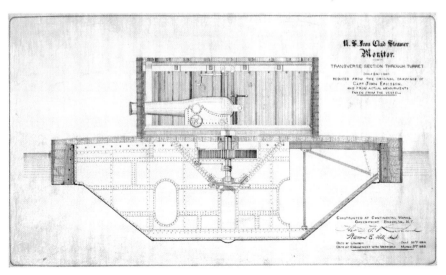

USS *Monitor*'s turret plans. *Courtesy of The Mariners' Museum.*

quite as sure of the ironclad, as Quartermaster Peter Truscott noted that "[s]he was a little bit the strangest craft I had ever seen."[15] Seaman David R. Ellis made perhaps the most telling remark about the *Monitor* as she readied to leave New York, commenting, "She had not been pronounced seaworthy, and no one could safely judge of her fighting qualities."[16]

On the afternoon of 6 March 1862, the USS *Monitor* left New York under tow by the steam tug *Seth Low*. The *Monitor* encountered severe storms off the New Jersey coast and almost sank en route to Hampton Roads. Somehow the little ironclad survived the angry sea. Lieutenant Samuel Dana Greene, the *Monitor*'s executive officer, later wrote about the stormy trip from New York, "I think I lived 10 good years."[17]

Battle of Hampton Roads map. *Courtesy of John Moran Quarstein.*

Battle of the ironclads. *Courtesy of Virginia War Museum.*

The Confederates were surprised when this "tin can on a shingle" approached their fire and blocked their path to the stranded frigate. For the next four hours, the *Monitor* and *Virginia* dueled, but neither ship was able to inflict serious damage to the other. The *Monitor* briefly broke off the engagement to resupply ammunition into her turret. The *Virginia* took this opportunity to move against the *Minnesota*; however, she ran aground. The Union ironclad approached and bombarded the *Virginia* until the Confederate ironclad was able to free herself. Jones then tried to ram the *Monitor*. The collision caused more damage to the Confederate vessel, as the *Virginia*'s wooden hull just glanced off the iron deck of the more nimble *Monitor*. When the Union ironclad tried to ram the *Virginia*'s rudder, a steering malfunction caused the *Monitor* to swerve away just as a shell struck the *Monitor*'s pilothouse, blinding Lieutenant Worden and causing the *Monitor* to temporarily break off action. Believing that the Union ironclad had had enough and suffering from several leaks, the *Virginia* returned to the Elizabeth River with the receding tide.

Both sides claimed victory. The *Monitor* was successful in stopping the Confederate ironclad from destroying the Federal wooden warships. Nevertheless, the *Virginia* blocked the James River and closed this approach toward Richmond to the Federal fleet. This strategic situation had a major impact on McClellan's plans to strike at Richmond.

A few days after the battle, McClellan inquired of the U.S. Navy whether or not he could "rely on the *Monitor* to keep the *Merrimack* in check, so that I can make Fort Monroe a base of operations?"[18] Gustavus Vasa Fox, assistant secretary of the navy, replied that he believed the *Monitor* to be superior to the *Merrimack* but that she might be damaged in the next encounter. "The *Monitor* may, and I think will, destroy the *Merrimack* in the next fight; but this is hope not certainty."[19] McClellan was concerned. "The performances of the *Merrimac* place a new aspect upon everything," McClellan wrote to General Wool, "and may very probably change my whole plan of campaign, just on the eve of execution."[20]

6

The Campaign Commences

The events of 8 and 9 March left an indelible mark on the strategic balance of the Peninsula. Even though the first engagement between ironclad vessels broke off in a draw, the check given to the *Virginia* by the *Monitor* relieved the Federals' fears of a broken blockade with Northern cities attacked. The battle, however, had even more immediate implications than being a major turning point in naval warfare, as the undefeated *Virginia* blocked the entrance to the James River and closed this approach to Richmond to the Federals. The mere existence of the *Virginia* would have a powerful influence on the campaign that was soon to begin on the Peninsula.

Simultaneously with the Confederate naval victory on 8 March, Joe Johnston abandoned his fortifications around Manassas and retreated to the Rappahannock River. This completely upset McClellan's plans, as a Union landing at Urbanna would no longer achieve the same strategic results. The Army of the Potomac made a brave march forward on 10 March and ventured into the Confederate defenses only to discover logs mounted as "Quaker Guns." Once again McClellan suffered an embarrassment, and Lincoln's confidence in his general-in-chief was eroded even further. The next day, the president relieved McClellan as general-in-chief of the Federal armies, but since his troops had finally taken the field, Lincoln retained Little Mac as commander of the Army of the Potomac. Lincoln believed that McClellan held too much responsibility and wanted the general to focus on the Army of the Potomac's drive against Richmond. The president actively assumed the role of commander-in-chief. McClellan, in turn, was greatly insulted by the political machinations "persecuting a man behind his back" but nevertheless was mollified by his continuance as Army of the Potomac commander.[1]

McClellan was committed to an amphibious operation and decided to proceed with his secondary concept: an advance against Richmond by way of the Peninsula. He believed that by using "Fort Monroe as a base," the Army of the Potomac could march against Richmond "with complete security, altho' with less celerity and brilliancy of results, up the Peninsula."[2] While his corps commanders all agreed to a new concept, there were serious concerns about the Confederate ironclad. The Army of the Potomac's Chief Engineer, Brigadier General John G. Barnard, believed that the *Virginia* "paralyzes the movement of this army by whatever route is adopted."[3] McClellan sought to allay these fears by contacting General Wool and Assistant Secretary of the Navy Gustavus Fox to obtain their opinions from Hampton Roads. Fox replied that "[t]he *Monitor* is more than a match for the *Merrimack*, but she might be disabled in the next encounter."[4] Wool concurred. He had already received orders on 9 March from McClellan to hold Fort Monroe "at all hazard" against the Confederate ironclad. Wool began work to block the *Virginia*'s access into the Chesapeake Bay by mounting a 15-inch Rodman gun, nicknamed the "Lincoln Gun," next to the 12-inch "Union Gun" on the beach in front of the Old Point Comfort Lighthouse. Wool was sure that the *Monitor*, supported by these two powerful guns, would effectively close the mouth of Hampton Roads to any sortie by the *Virginia*. Even though the *Virginia* still blocked the James River to his use, McClellan believed that with naval support, he could open the York River by overrunning the Confederate positions at Yorktown and Gloucester Point and then on to West Point and Richmond. McClellan advised Lincoln on 13 March that he intended "to take the field immediately upon arriving at Fort Monroe…by rapid movements to drive before me, or capture the enemy on the peninsula, open the James River, and push on to Richmond before he could be materially reinforced from other portions of his territory."[5]

Even before McClellan left for the Peninsula, he realized that the anticipated naval assistance would not be as extensive as originally planned. Goldsborough had previously advised McClellan that his primary duty was to neutralize the *Merrimack* and that he could only provide the support of several wooden gunboats. These warships were perceived as an inadequate force to combat the heavy Confederate water batteries at Yorktown and Gloucester Point. Magruder had striven to close his York River flank and made his water batteries as powerful as possible. Yorktown water batteries generally had eighteen-foot parapets, and all the guns were positioned en barbette. The works included traverses between the guns, along with well-constructed magazines and bombproofs. There were seven individual water batteries, armed as follows:

- No. 1: five 8-inch Columbiads
- No. 2: four 8-inch Columbiads
- No. 3: three 32-pounder Columbiads and one 32-pounder naval gun
- No. 4: three 32-pounder Columbiads (1827 Pattern)
- No. 5: two 32-pounder Columbiads
- No. 6: three IX-inch Dahlgrens
- No. 7: three 8-inch Columbiads and one 64-pounder

This battery, built on the beach beneath the cliff, also included a 42-pounder carronade to sweep the shore, helping to repel any amphibious assault.

The main works on the heights contained heavy guns, rifled 24- and 18-pounders, to help repel naval attack and provide counter-battery fire against the enemy's siege works. The Gloucester Point batteries were equally extensive. The water battery was built just two feet above sea level, designed to mount twelve IX-inch Dahlgrens positioned en barbette. This battery

High Redoubt, Yorktown, Virginia, May 1862. *Courtesy of the U.S. Army Military Historical Institute.*

Union gunboats shelling Yorktown and Gloucester Point, April 1862, Robert Sneden. *Courtesy of the Virginia Historical Society.*

included bombproofs, magazines and a hot-shot furnace. It was connected by a covered way to a large covering work, forty feet above the sea face on a bluff. This earthwork also contained Dahlgrens and other heavy ordnance to provide plunging fire against any naval force attempting to pass the narrows between Yorktown and Gloucester Point.

Consequently, McClellan had already recognized the need to counter the Confederate hold on the York River narrows (the river was less than half a mile wide between Yorktown and Gloucester Point). He therefore began considering besieging Yorktown on 20 March, as he wrote that the "first operation will be the capture of Yorktown & Gloucester, this may involve a siege (at least I go prepared for one) in case the Navy is not able to afford the means of destroying the rebel batteries at these points."[6]

George McClellan had witnessed the effect of coastal sieges before when he served as an engineer under Winfield Scott constructing batteries at Vera Cruz, and he made observations of the siege of Sebastapol during the Crimean War. The siege train included some of the most powerful weapons in the world, including 8-, 10- and 13-inch seacoast mortars, as well as 30-, 100- and 200-pounder Parrott rifles. Obviously, McClellan knew that his arsenal could, if necessary, utterly destroy the Confederate positions defending the York River. The possibility of a siege did not bother McClellan. He believed that he could use General McDowell's I Corps to envelop the Confederate Gloucester Point defenses, an act that would turn all of the Confederate defenses in the region. McClellan thought that a second siege of Yorktown would achieve the same goal as Washington's siege of Cornwallis in 1781: the utter defeat of the enemy.

Endeavoring to fulfill President Lincoln's order of 8 March that McClellan begin his campaign within ten days, on 17 March the Army of the Potomac began its grand movement to the Peninsula. In less than three weeks, 389 vessels delivered the following to Fort Monroe and Camp Butler: 121,500 men, 14,592 animals, 1,224 vehicles, 44 artillery batteries "and the enormous quantity of equipage…required for an army of such magnitude."[7] The Army of the Potomac commander knew that he could, after the capture of Yorktown, create a base near West Point, Virginia, the terminus of the Richmond & York River Railroad, to make his final advance on the Confederate capital, so he ordered locomotives and cars to operate on the captured railway. To move all these men and material, McClellan organized a transportation fleet of 113 steamers, as well as 276 sailing vessels and canalboats, at a cost of more than $24,300 per day. As McClellan's army began to arrive on the Peninsula, Hampton Roads became filled with this vast armada of vessels. The new camp created outside Fort Monroe and Camp Butler became the largest city in the South. The men were overjoyed to finally be on the move against the Confederates and were confident of victory. McClellan announced to his men as they prepared to leave their camps around Washington: "The moment for action has arrived, and I know that I can trust in you to save our country…I will bring you face to face with the rebels…where I know you wish to be…on the decisive battlefield."[8] Waiting for this massive force was John Bankhead Magruder's thirteen-thousand-strong Army of the Peninsula. Magruder had been aware of the steady buildup of Union troops on the Peninsula since "the glorious achievement of the Confederate States war-steamer *Virginia*." In fact, he had anticipated this circumstance when he reported to Richmond a day after the 9 March engagement that "[f]inding, as I anticipated that the naval attack produced no effect upon the fort except to increase its garrison, I contended myself with occupying the most advanced posts, Bethel and Young's Mill where the troops are now."[9] Magruder, nonetheless, kept his soldiers at work improving every aspect of his Peninsula defenses. Lieutenant Robert Miller of the 2nd Louisiana wrote that "General Magruder has caused all of the roads to be blockaded between our lines and Newport News, so that it is next thing to impossibility for anyone to get along much less an army. The state of inactivity we have been in has been very harassing to us but we have spent it profitably and our Reg. has done more work than any two others on the Peninsula."[10]

Confederate engineers also sought ways to enhance Magruder's river flanks. Even though the *Virginia*'s mere existence blocked the James River to the Union, "ironclad fever" had spread throughout the command, and engineers identified the best method to defend land batteries against the possible advance of the *Monitor* or any other Federal ironclads. Alfred Rives, acting chief of the Engineer Bureau, reported:

> *The recent conflict at Newport News shows conclusively that water-batteries, especially those near deep water, cannot inure materially properly constructed iron-clad vessels, nor contend with them…The only point on the Peninsula where I think casemates of value is Mulberry Island Point. The enemy cannot approach that point nearer than about half a mile, and properly constructed casemates may resist their fire at that distance.*[11]

Confederate engineers set forth, quickly rebuilding the defenses on Mulberry Island. Mulberry Island Point Battery had five 42-pounders mounted, and fourteen casemates were under construction. Bombproofs were added to Fort Crafford. Robert E. Lee, now serving as Jefferson Davis's military advisor, urged the work forward as Rives wrote to Captain John J. Clarke, the engineer in charge of battery construction at Mulberry Island Point:

> *It seems almost needless to urge upon you the vigorous prosecution of the works at Mulberry Point, but I do so at the suggestion of General Lee, who thinks it a matter of paramount importance. I received to-day a telegram from General Magruder to effect that he had directed you to place the 42 and 68 pounders in barbette in the work surrounding Crafford's house. In this, from the lights before me, I should think the general probably right. The work on the point can then be prosecuted untrammeled by guns in position.*
>
> *I send you to-day 1,000 sand bags, and you will receive with this letter the first installment of bolts for the casemate battery. I have been trying in vain, so far, to procure wrought-iron protection for the embrasures, but think that I have succeeded to-day in making a plan and procuring flat-bar railroad iron from the Richmond and Danville Railroad Company which will be perfectly satisfactory. A tracing will be sent to you to-morrow. I shall write a note this evening to Colonel Gorgas requesting him to send you immediately a 6.4 inch rifle gun, 64-pounder, Columbiad pattern, with barbette carriage pintle-block, which is here on hand complete. One casemate carriage will be finished this week and five the next, if promises may be relied on.*
>
> *General Lee is particularly desirous that all your unmounted guns should be mounted immediately, and in the present state of affairs I do not think*

you can do better than to mount them all in the covering works around Crafford's house. On that, however, you will probably be the best judge.[12]

In addition to the Mulberry Island battery, Major General Benjamin Huger, an 1825 West Point graduate who had served as General Scott's chief of ordnance in Mexico, had fortified the south side of the James (which formed part of his Department of Norfolk) with two earthen fortifications. These water batteries were known as Fort Boykin and Fort Huger. Fort Boykin was originally built in 1623 on Day's Point by Roger Smith to defend Virginia from Spanish and Indian attacks, and it was called "Castle at the Rocks." Renamed Fort Boykin in honor of Revolutionary War officer Major Francis Boykin, the fort was expanded into a seven-pointed, star-shaped fort on its land face during the War of 1812 and was once again improved in 1861. Fort Boykin was armed with ten 42-pounder and 32-pounder cannons.

A few miles up the James River was Fort Huger. Sited on Hardy's Bluff, directly across the river from Mulberry Island, Fort Huger was built in 1861 under the guidance of 1818 West Point graduate Colonel Andrew Talcott. The fort was named in honor of General Huger and mounted thirteen guns, including one 10-inch rifled Columbiad, four rifled IX-inch Dahlgrens, two 8-inch rifled Columbiads and six 32-pounder hot-shot guns. Fort Huger had a hot-shot furnace that made shot red hot to fire at warships as they endeavored to steam past the fort. Unfortunately, General Robert E. Lee noted that Hardy's (also referred to as Hardin's or Harden's) Bluff was "not in good defensive position,"[13] as not all of its cannons were mounted, bombproofs constructed and traverses built. This work was completed by early April 1862 due to the efforts of Acting Chief Engineer Alfred Rives.

By mid-March, it became obvious that the Federals intended to march up the Peninsula toward Richmond rather than attempt, as the Confederates had supposed, an attack against Norfolk. Wool's command now numbered over thirteen thousand troops, and on 14 March, Magruder reported that the Federals were becoming aggressive, pressuring the Confederate pickets on the Warwick Road. Prince John was anxious, and on 10 March, he warned Richmond:

The enemy again drove in the pickets to-day on the Warwick road after exchanging fire. He appears to be operating with a considerable advance guard, supported by heavier bodies, between it and Newport News, so that it is difficult to cut off the advance troops without entangling my handful of men with very superior numbers lying in wait…So, if the enemy persevere,

I shall be compelled in a very short time to withdraw the regiments which are now in front of the second, viz, from Yorktown to Mulberry Island.[14]

The Army of the Peninsula was now beginning to receive a trickle of reinforcements; however, the additional troops and supplies did not mollify Magruder's belief that his army was in an increasingly tenuous situation. He once again advised Richmond:

I have prepared as my real line of defense positions at Harwood's and Young's Mills...In my opinion, this advance line...might have been held by 20,000 troops...Finding my forces too weak to attempt defense of this line, I was compelled to prepare to receive the enemy on a second line, on Warwick River. Keeping then only small bodies of troops at Harwood's and Young's mills.[15]

Robert E. Lee agreed with Magruder's assessment and advised him:

A defensive line between Yorktown and Mulberry Island by damming and defending the Warwick River promises the happiest results. I would therefore recommend to you, should you concur in this opinion, to apply as great a force on the work as possible. With your left flank resting on the York River and your right defended by the batteries on James River, with the aid of the Virginia and other steamers, I think you may defy the advance of the enemy of the Peninsula, supported as this line would be by your second system of defenses.[16]

Lee later added that the Warwick Line "can be best held as long as your flanks are not turned by the passage of the enemy up either river. If you abandon that line, I know no better position you could assume on the Peninsula."[17] Magruder complied with Lee's directive but continued to fret about the growing Union presence. He bombarded Richmond constantly with letters and telegrams for more men and artillery, to the extent that Lee chided him for his repetitive requests. The Confederate general believed that he had little hope of holding Yorktown against the Federal onslaught. His defenses mounted eighty-five heavy guns and fifty-five field pieces, but he had insufficient manpower to hold both his river defenses and the twelve-mile line between Mulberry Island and Yorktown. Magruder continued to improve his defensive position as he awaited the Federal juggernaut. Private Edward Seton noted in March 1862 that "[a]ppearances here are quite changed. Here all the breast-works have been renewed and all the timber cut down."[18] Magruder advised Lee that "I have made arrangements to fight with my small force, but without the slightest hope of success." While he admitted doubt to Richmond, Prince John did not reveal his fears to his own troops. He issued a patriotic call to repel "the ruthless tyrants," advising his Army of the Peninsula that "these frowning battlements on the heights of York are turned in this second war of liberty against the enemies of our country."[19] On 28 March 1862, Magruder once again wrote to his troops: "The enemy is at length advancing. We shall fight him on the line of the Warwick River."[20]

General Robert E. Lee, CSA. *Courtesy of the Museum of the Confederacy.*

The Army of the Peninsula had made its final arrangements for defending this avenue to Richmond by 1 April 1862. Magruder later reported on his defenses:

> *The Warwick Line, upon which we rested, may be briefly described as follows: Warwick river rises…about a mile and a half to the right of Yorktown. Yorktown and Redoubts Nos. 4 and 5, united by long curtains and flanked by rifled pits from the left of the line until…it reaches the Warwick River…a sluggish and boggy stream, 20 or 30 yards wide… running through a dense wood fringed by swamps. Along this river are five dams; one at Wynn's Mill, one at Lee's Mill, and three constructed by myself. The effect of these dams is to back up to the water along the course of the river, so that for nearly three-fourths of its distance its passage is impracticable for either artillery or infantry. Each of these dams is protected by artillery and extensive earthworks for infantry.*[21]

Magruder thought that the Warwick-Yorktown Line had several weak points along his defensive system. And one area of concern was between the deep ravines leading to the headwaters of the Warwick River and

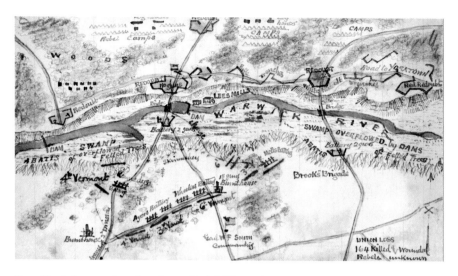

Dam No. 1, incorrectly referred to as Lee's Mill, April 1862, Robert Sneden. *Courtesy of the Virginia Historical Society.*

Yorktown. Accordingly, Magruder constructed two large earthworks known as the Red and White Redoubts. The White Redoubt was also called Fort Magruder. This lunette was armed with several heavy siege guns and field pieces, including one 8-inch Columbiad, one 42-pounder Columbiad and one 8-inch siege howitzer. These redoubts were connected and supported by trenches and redans.

A majority of Magruder's slender force, now numbering eleven thousand men, was positioned along the Warwick. His troop dispositions left six thousand men holding the garrisons at Gloucester Point, Yorktown and Mulberry Island. The balance of the line was defended by five thousand men. Troops were, however, arriving from Richmond as reinforcements even before McClellan began his advance. The 9th Alabama arrived at Lebanon Church after a boat trip down from Richmond to King's Mill Wharf. The march to the Warwick Line was difficult, as Edmund Dewitt Patterson recounted that it was "a march that beggars description. The night was so dark that it was impossible to see anything...The mud and water was literally knee deep...Some men fell in mudholes and had to be dragged out."[22] Magruder maintained a small advance force at Howard's Bridge and Young's Mill. The Union troops were already making strong reconnaissance up the Peninsula to "ascertain the position and strength of the enemy."[23]

Even though the reconnaissance of Brigadier General William F. "Baldy" Smith's division "gained information that the enemy held Young's Mill in strong force," it was actually only held by two regiments commanded by Brigadier General Lafayette McLaws. Magruder was just beginning his ruse of strength, and it was working. "I wish Young's Mill held to the last without fighting for it," Prince John commented, as "I am maneuvering to give the enemy the idea we are in great force."[24]

George McClellan arrived on the Peninsula on 2 April 1862, aboard his steamer *Commodore*, happy to be free of "that sink of inequity," Washington.[25] His demotion from general-in-chief to just commander of the Army of the Potomac made him now determined to achieve success. The Army of the Potomac's Chief Engineer Brigadier General John Gross Barnard lobbied McClellan to attack and capture Norfolk first. This action would eliminate the Confederate ironclad and open the James River, thus avoiding the need to besiege Yorktown. Barnard was a brilliant officer. An 1833 West Point graduate, he had taught twice at the academy and served as the USMA's superintendent. When war erupted, he was chief engineer of Washington and personally planned the Union army's approach against the Confederate positions along Bull Run. The author of *Notes on Seacoast Defense*, Barnard believed that Norfolk

Confederate Yorktown defenses. *Courtesy of the U.S. Army Military Historical Institute.*

was the key to the campaign's success. Despite this sound advice, McClellan decided to march against Yorktown and Gloucester Point and then establish his base at West Point for his attack on Richmond. He knew that once past Yorktown, Norfolk would fall under Union control. McClellan again tried to enlist the cooperation of Flag Officer Louis M. Goldsborough's fleet to quicken the capture of the Confederate York River defenses, but the Federal fleet was too occupied with the *Virginia* to mount an expedition against the Gloucester Point batteries. Without naval participation and additional troops, McClellan still believed that he could take Yorktown through a brief siege. McClellan was angered by the lack of support. He believed the withholding of Brigadier General Irvin McDowell's I Corps was a "fatal error." He was convinced that the lack of these troops made it impossible for him to complete his plan for a "rapid and brilliant operation." The Army of the Potomac commander later wrote, "I know of no instance in military history where a general in the field has received such a discouraging blow."[26] McClellan blamed it on the abolitionist politicians in Washington.

McClellan still endeavored to secure more men before he launched his troops up the Peninsula. Wool's command, headquartered at Fort Monroe, contained more than ten thousand soldiers and was initially placed under McClellan's jurisdiction. Just as he sought to assign them to his army, the order was countermanned. McClellan was immediately incensed: "I was deprived of all control over General Wool and the troops under his command, and forbidden to detach any of his troops without his sanction. This order left me without any base of operations under my own control, and to this day, I am ignorant of the causes which led to it."[27]

Although the septuagenarian Wool, a brevet major general since the Mexican War, may have considered McClellan somewhat of an upstart, the commander of the Union Department of Virginia agreed that he would lend McClellan whatever support he required. Other than maps, information about the Confederate positions on the Peninsula and camping dispositions for his own troops as they arrived in Hampton Roads, McClellan never called on Wool for any other assistance.

Since the James River was declared by the naval authorities closed to the operations of their vessels by the combined influence of the enemy's batteries on its banks and the Confederate steamers *Virginia*, *Yorktown*, *Jamestown* and *Teaser*, McClellan resolved to flank the Confederates out of their positions at Yorktown, thereby opening the James River with a Southern retreat. McClellan's information, provided by Allan Pinkerton and Major General John E. Wool, indicated that Magruder's force of fifteen thousand

Major General John Ellis Wool, USA. *Courtesy of The Casemate Museum.*

to twenty thousand men was at Yorktown, with his right flank unsecured. The Federal commander thought that he could interpose his troops across the Confederate line of retreat, trapping Prince John at Yorktown like Washington had cornered Cornwallis. Maps provided by General Wool indicated good roads and no water barriers, so McClellan seemed confident of a quick victory on the Lower Peninsula. Brigadier General Samuel P. Heintzelman's III Corps, followed by elements of Brigadier General Edwin Vose Sumner's II Corps, was to march on the Hampton-York Road through Big Bethel directly to Yorktown to hold Magruder in his defenses. McClellan believed that Heintzelman's advance would flank the Confederates out of their Young's Mill strong point. The path would then be clear for Brigadier General Erasmus Darwin Keyes's IV Corps to march up the Warwick Road through Warwick Court House to the Half-Way House northwest of Yorktown, thereby cutting the Confederate line of retreat.

McClellan was not pleased with his corps commanders and felt that "many of the difficulties and delays grew out of the fact that I could not trust any of the Corps Commanders."[28] The corps structure had been forced on McClellan, and the initial commanders were all seasoned veterans with greater seniority than the Army of the Potomac's commander. Brigadier General Edwin Vose Sumner was sixty-five years old and had served in the U.S. Army since 1819, fighting with distinction in the Black Hawk and Mexican Wars. Nicknamed "Bull" for his booming voice and noted for his bravery in battle, he had been promoted far above his ability as commander of II Corps. McClellan noted that Sumner was "in many respects…a model soldier, but unfortunately nature has limited his capacity to a very narrow extent."[29] Brigadier General Samuel Peter Heintzelman was an 1826 West Point graduate who had received brevets while fighting in Mexico and against the Indians. He had argued against the Urbanna Plan. The other corps commander to go to the Peninsula with McClellan was Erasmus Darwin Keyes. Keyes, an 1832 West Point graduate, had previously served as a member of the USMA Board of Visitors, and he also taught at the academy. He served as Winfield Scott's aide-de-camp on two occasions, and when the war erupted, he was the commanding general's military secretary. He then helped dispatch troops from New York to Washington, D.C., and to Fort Monroe, and he commanded a brigade during the Battle of First Manassas.

The Union army began its march on 4 April 1862. Keyes's IV Corps left Newport News Point with Brigadier General Baldy Smith's division, supported by the 5th U.S. Cavalry, in the advance. The Federals brushed aside Confederate pickets at Water's Creek and prepared to encounter the Southern "strong works and... force at Young's Mill." When Smith's division reached the mill, "the enemy retreated at our approach," Keyes reported, "firing only a few shots."[30] The IV Corps had reached its goal for the first day's march without any bloodshed. Keyes's troops were amazed at the extensive Confederate works at Young's Mill. Private Wilbur Fisk of the 2nd Vermont recalled, "We drove the enemy from a position they had fortified and that night occupied the place ourselves. The rebels left quite a village of huts or barracks, and from appearances, they had enjoyed much more comfortable quarters during the winter than we had

Brigadier General Eramus Darwin Keyes, USA. *Courtesy of the U.S. Army Military Historical Institute.*

ourselves."[31] The IV Corps' commander was happy that the Confederates had not made a more resolute stand at Young's Mill, as Keyes reported to General McClellan that "the enemy's work at Young's Mill are so strong, that with 5,000 men he might have stopped my two divisions there a week."[32] The Confederate works at Young's Mill were very extensive, as Lieutenant Charles Harvey Brewster of the 10th Massachusetts Volunteers wrote:

> *The road went down in a sort of ravine, and right across from the dam on one side to the bank on the other was a line of logs about 4 inches in diameter and firmly planted in the ground close together and about 10 feet height cut off and sharpened to a point. Where the road went through there was a strong gate, right behind this a high bank, crowned by a fort with embrasures for two guns. There every knoll was crowned by a breastwork for rifle men and stretching away as far as we could see were breastworks with embrasures for cannon, and behind these were the Barracks, enough to contain 4 or 5,000 soldiers.*[33]

It was the same story at Big Bethel on the Hampton-York Road. Heintzelman's III Corps had taken the lead from Hampton marching

Confederate defenses at Young's Mill, 4 April 1862. *Courtesy of the Vermont Historical Society.*

toward Yorktown. The troops had expected a strong defense at the scene of the Union defeat the year before, but instead of a "line of fire run along their breastworks...Not a sound came from them and not a man could we see," recounted Private Oliver W. Norton of the 83rd Pennsylvania Infantry. "We came up to the front and our color guard leaped the ditch and planted the flag of the Eighty-third on the fortifications so long disgraced by the rebel rag. Great Bethel was ours and not a man hurt."[34]

Magruder's first defensive line impressed all the Federal soldiers, yet they were vacant. Keyes believed that had the position been held by the Confederates, it could have required a siege of two weeks to capture the Young's Mill defenses. Consequently, the Union army had made good progress on 4 April, and from Young's Mill, Keyes expected to be able to reach the Half-Way House on the morrow.

The IV Corps began its march at 6:00 a.m. on 5 April. Smith's division once again led the march. At 7:00 a.m., it began to rain, "pouring in torrents, rendering the roads well-nigh impassable,"[35] which slowed the troops' progress. Then, at about 11:00 a.m., the march was stopped by a large force of Confederates occupying a strong position at the Lee's Mill crossing of the Warwick River. Lee's Mill, the Warwick River's course across the Peninsula and the Confederate fortifications were not noted on the maps available to the Union command. The Federals were shocked by the "very serious resistance they encountered at Lee's Mill. Flames appeared on all sides," reported Baldy Smith as his men approached the river. He was forced to advise Keyes that "we shall not be able to reach the Half-Way House on the Yorktown-Williamsburg Road today."[36]

The crossing at Lee's Mill was held by about 1,800 Confederates, including Colonel Alfred Cumming's 10th Georgia and several batteries, under the overall command of Brigadier General Lafayette McLaws. McLaws, an 1842 West Point graduate from Georgia, had served during the Mexican War and on the Utah Expedition. Lee's Mill was considered a "naturally strong position" by Magruder's chief of artillery, Colonel Henry Coulter Cabell, a graduate of the University of Virginia and prewar lawyer from Richmond. All the approaches to this milldam crossing were covered by redoubts constructed along the millpond or overlooking the Warwick as it "follows a tortuous course through salt marshes…from which the land rises up boldly to a height of 30 or 40 feet."[37] Redoubts dotted the front lines at Lee's Mill and were manned by several batteries, including local artillerists serving in Captain Joseph B. Cosnahan's Peninsula Artillery from the 1st Virginia Regiment. Commanding two of Cosnahan's guns (a 10-pounder Parrott rifle and a 12-pounder Napoleon smoothbore) at Lee's Mill was former Warwick County clerk of the court and College of William and Mary graduate, 1st Lieutenant William B. Jones. Jones's cannon fire helped

Union Army of the Potomac advancing through Big Bethel fortifications, 4 April 1862. *Courtesy of the Virginia War Museum.*

to repulse the initial Union assault. Agitated by continued Federal counter-battery fire, Jones returned fire so hot that the Northern battery, Captain Charles Wheeler's Battery E, 1st New York Light Artillery, quickly retreated out of range. His spirited leadership at Lee's Mill reportedly earned him the nickname of "Hell Cat Billy" and a promotion as Colonel Cabell's adjutant.

Faced by such determined resistance that magnified the strength of the Confederate defenses, Keyes realized that his flanking movement to trap Magruder at Yorktown was stymied. He wrote McClellan from his headquarters at Warwick Court House, "Magruder is in a strongly fortified position behind the Warwick River, the fords to which have been destroyed by dams, and the approaches to which are through dense forests, swamps, and marshes. No part of this line as discovered can be taken without an enormous waste of life."[38]

General Barnard concurred with Keyes's assessment and remarked that "the line is certainly one of the most extensive known to modern times." Barnard was astounded that "within twelve miles of the outposts troops under [McClellan's] command a powerful defensive line had been thrown during the winter and spring, of which he knew nothing whatever. Though it lay across his meditated line of march."[39]

The Army of the Potomac's chief engineer was also displeased with the poor maps of the Peninsula provided by General Wool's topographical engineer, Lieutenant Colonel Thomas Jefferson Cram. Cram had incorrectly charted the Warwick River to turn northwest at Lee's Mill to create Mulberry Island. This peninsula, bounded by the Warwick River, James River and Skiffes Creek, was called an island but was not. Instead, the Warwick River reached almost to Yorktown and was transformed into a major defensive barrier by the Confederates. McClellan had thought that the James and York Rivers would aid his advance; however, the Tidewater geography witnessed numerous tributaries flowing across the Peninsula that actually retarded his advance. Wool's engineer reported that the two main roads to be used by the Federals, Hampton Road (also known as the Great Warwick) and Hampton-York Road, were in good condition. These roads may have been good for the local population of about seven thousand people, but they collapsed under the weight of the thousands of Union soldiers marching on them in the heavy rain. Major Charles Wainwright studied the consistency of the roads and noted that there was a foot or so of sandy loam, which sat on shell marl that rested on a subsoil of heavy clay. Since the roads were not crowned nor did they have ditches to facilitate water runoff, the water went right to the subsoil, turning it into "the consistency of soft mortar." Wainwright,

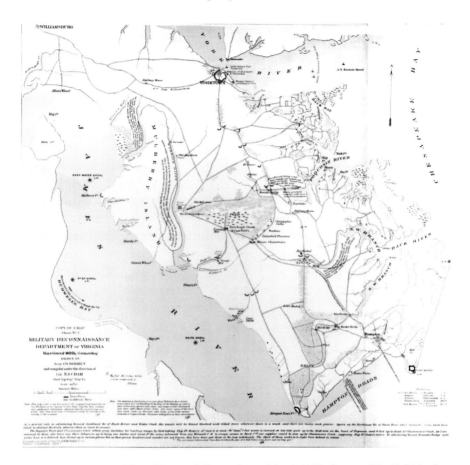

Lower Peninsula map, Major Thomas Jefferson Cram, March 1862. *Courtesy of Lee Hall Mansion.*

consequently, noted that whenever the surface crust was broken, "there is nothing to stop its sinking until it reaches the hard clay."[40] Rain turned the roads into quagmires, and this circumstance plagued both armies. The lack of knowledge of what lay before truly altered McClellan's plans. Lee's Mill, noted McClellan, was "incapable of being carried by assault."[41] The brief engagement at Lee's Mill cost the Confederates seven casualties and the Union twelve. It had far-reaching implications. Halted before the unexpected array of enemy entrenchment, McClellan resolved to deploy the 101 heavy guns he had brought to the Peninsula and lay siege to Magruder's defenses.

McClellan's hesitation at the Warwick River set the stage for a carefully organized Confederate ruse. Magruder began shuttling his soldiers to and fro to create the illusion of many troops arriving on this line and moving into positions of great strength. Private Edmund Dewitt Patterson of the 9th Alabama wrote that he and his fellow Confederate soldiers "have been traveling most of the day…with no other view than to show ourselves to the enemy, at as many different points of the line as possible."[42] Lieutenant James Miller of the 14th Louisiana reflected that they had marched back and forth from the James River to the York River six times as he explained Magruder's ruse in a letter home: "The way Magruder fooled them was to divide each body of his troops into two parts and keep them traveling all the time for twenty-four hours, til reinforcements came."[43] Magruder earned the title "Master of Ruses and Strategy" for his make-believe show of strength, constantly "[b]ringing in regiments from less exposed positions on the line, marched them in a circle, as it were, all day emerging from the woods on one part of the line, into the wood below, then on a 'Double quick' behind the hill and woods to appear again as fresh troops arriving," as Corporal J.W. Minnish wrote.[44] "It was a wonderful thing," recorded diarist Mary Chesnut, "how he played his ten thousand before McClellan like fireflies and utterly deluded him."[45]

Gloucester Point fortifications, May 1862. *Courtesy of the U.S. Army Military Historical Institute.*

Confederate fortifications at Dam No. 1, May 1862. *Courtesy of the Vermont Historical Society.*

Despite outnumbering Magruder almost four to one, McClellan soon became convinced that he faced more than 100,000 Confederates. McClellan just could not rationalize that any smaller force would dare defend such a twelve-mile front. The fifth of April was simply a bad day for McClellan. His plans for a rapid movement past Yorktown against Richmond were upset not only by the unexpected Confederate defenses but also by Lincoln's decision not to release elements of Major General Irvin McDowell's I Corps from northern Virginia to use to turn the Confederate York River defenses. The U.S. Navy once again refused to attempt any offensive action in either the James or York Rivers because of the CSS *Virginia*. Since neither the navy nor Lincoln would provide him with the support necessary to assault Gloucester Point, thereby uncovering the Confederate defenses, McClellan believed that he had no other alternative that he was well prepared for except siege warfare.

The sixth of April was a day of reconnaissance. Thaddeus Lowe's balloon, *Intrepid*, made its first appearance over the Confederate lines. Many Federal officers wanted to know what was behind Magruder's brave front of frowning forts. Union field artillery was brought into position and opened fire on the enemy's position at Lee's Mill, then limbered and moved to another nearby field to repeat the action. Confederate counter-fire often forced the Federals to find cover, which would prompt loud cheers from the Southerners. Infantry units skirmished up and down the line simply to draw a response "while engineers and scouts observed and reported," as Lieutenant Edgar N. Newcomb of the 19th Massachusetts wrote his sister.[46] Private Patrick Lyons of the 2nd Rhode Island recorded in his diary that "all the action was only to gain the feel of the enemy and find out what force they had here, not to bring on an engagement."[47]

Baldy Smith, however, believed the line to be weaker than what met the eye. He ordered Brigadier General Winfield Scott Hancock to investigate the Warwick River defenses between Lee's Mill and Dam No. 1. As Hancock began to initiate his reconnaissance in force, McClellan ordered that no advances were to be made against the enemy until engineers had thoroughly studied the Confederate line. The attack, which Smith believed was a sure success, was called off. McClellan decided to ignore this possible avenue of attack almost simultaneously with his receipt of Lincoln's telegram urging him to "break the enemies' lines from York-town to Warwick River at once. They will probably use time, as advantageously as you can."[48] Little Mac paid little attention to Lincoln's advice, writing to his wife, "I was much tempted to reply that he had better come and do it himself." McClellan was committed to a siege and determined to avoid "the faults of the Allies at Sebastapol and quietly preparing the way for a great success."[49]

A "Dam Failure"

M agruder was amazed by the Union response to his bold, yet weak, defensive line and once again became a hero of the Southland. "The assuming and maintaining the line by Magruder, with his small force in the face of such overwhelming odds," wrote Brigadier General Jubal A. Early, "was one of the boldest exploits ever performed by a military commander."[1] Prince John, however, soon realized why McClellan hesitated to attack. He wrote Richmond that McClellan, "to my utter surprise…permitted day after day to elapse without an assault. In a few days the object of his delay was apparent. In every direction; in front of our lines; the intervening woods, and along the open fields, earthworks began to appear."[2]

Once his engineers conducted their surveys of the Confederate defenses, McClellan decided to concentrate his siege engineering on Yorktown. His plan was to assault the Confederate works in the vicinity of the historic town once his heavy artillery had breached them. Little Mac laid out fourteen batteries and three redoubts for the heavy 8-, 10- and 13-inch seacoast mortars and the enormous 100- and 200-pounder Parrott guns, as well as 20- and 30-pounder Parrotts and 4.5-inch Rodman siege rifles that he had brought to the Peninsula. The Army of the Potomac commander established a debarkation base at Wormley Creek to unload and move into forward positions the 101 siege guns he had brought with him to the Peninsula. It was a herculean effort.

However, once in a battery, a 13-inch seacoast mortar weighing seventeen thousand pounds could hurl a two-hundred-pound explosive shell with a twenty-pound powder charge 4,325 yards when elevated at forty-five degrees. These mortars were brought up Wormley Creek on canalboats. The boats' sides were cut down so that the mortars and their iron carriages could be hoisted, dragged ashore on rollers and then moved to their battery under a high-wheeled sling cart. Nearly 5,000 yards of roads, as well as three pontoon bridges, two long crib-work bridges to cross ravines and one floating raft bridge and other small crossings were constructed to move all the equipment, ammunition (six hundred wagons of powder, shot and shell) and guns into position. The batteries were skillfully arranged with great precision by General Barnard to provide direct and indirect fire on the Confederate water batteries, Red Redoubt, Fort Magruder (White Redoubt) and Wynne's Mill. The large rifle guns could strike with pinpoint accuracy, while the mortars provided vertical fire. Once the bombardment began, the Confederates would have nowhere to hide from the seven thousand pounds per salvo pounding them. Batteries No. 1 and No. 4 were typical of the siege works. No. 1 was located in front of the Farinholt House on the right bank of Wormley Creek where it emptied into the York River. This battery commanded the waterfront of Yorktown and Gloucester Point. The 1st Connecticut Artillery manned this battery, which contained two 200-pounder and five 100-pounder Parrott rifles. Battery No. 4, also manned by the 1st Connecticut, was sited in a ravine near the Moore House and contained ten 13-inch seacoast mortars. This battery was capable of bombarding all the key Confederate positions from Wynne's Mill (4,900 yards away) to Gloucester Point (4,100 yards away). The Army of the Potomac's batteries featured the largest array of heavy artillery ever assembled in a siege.

McClellan named Brigadier General Fitz-John Porter as the director of siege operations and Captain James C. Duane, U.S. Engineer Corps, as superintendent for the construction of the siege works. Fitz-John Porter, an 1845 West Point graduate, fought in the Mexican War and served as an instructor at West Point. James Chatham Duane was an 1848 West Point graduate. He had spent most of his prewar career teaching engineering at the academy and supervising harbor improvements. Both Duane and Porter had served on the Utah Expedition and were friends of McClellan's. Union soldiers were now put to work under constant fire from the Confederate lines building the roads, rifle pits and gun emplacements necessary to eventually pound the Confederates into submission. Thomas B. Leaver of New Hampshire wrote, "It seems the fight has to be won partially through the implements of peace, the shovel, axe and pick."[3] Other soldiers commented

Farinholt House, Yorktown, Virginia, April 1862. *Courtesy of the U.S. Army Military Historical Institute.*

about the difficult work, noting the unusual sight of thousands of men at work in the darkness, "like a train of busy ants...shoveling away with now and then a shell bursting near,"[4] as Gilbert Thompson recorded in his diary.

Across the Warwick River from Mulberry Island, Brigadier General John J. Peck had his men very busy constructing rifle pits and batteries. Their work, however, was often disrupted by "the enemy's vessels," Peck noted, as the Southern gunboats "could control the navigation and reach our lines with heavy guns." Peck requested heavy artillery, "a small number (say two) of 8-inch howitzers and two 8-inch mortars," to contest Confederate control of the mouth of the Warwick. He asked McClellan, "Would not possession of the island enable the commanding general to control in a considerable degree the James River in case the Navy fails to do the work?" McClellan replied to Peck's superior, General Keyes, with the terse comment, "I think more heavy artillery necessary to make much impression to Mulberry Island

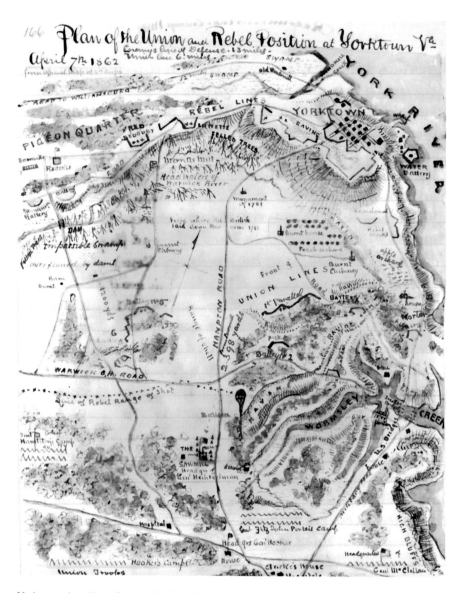

Yorktown siege lines, Robert Sneden, May 1862. *Courtesy of the Virginia Historical Society.*

than General Peck specifies." The Union commander seemed willing to ignore opportunities along the Warwick and focused on the completion of his siege lines.[5]

Observing all the immense labor by their Northern counterparts, Confederate soldiers expected an assault at any time. Surgeon James

Holloway of the 18th Mississippi wondered, "Why they do not attack us is strange for they have a heavy force and every day's delay only gives us the opportunity to strengthen our defenses."[6] Magruder countered, as "[h]is men and a considerable body of Negro laborers had been and still were engaged in strengthening the works by working night and day," Jubal Early later wrote, "so that their energies were taxed to the utmost limit."[7] Yet Prince John carried off his charade of a powerful army and buoyed his troops' morale in the grand fashion that only he could exhibit. "When Magruder's cavalcade at a full gallop inspected the thin lines of the Warwick, it was a sight for men and gods," Moxley Sorrel wrote. "Of commanding form and loving display, he had assembled a numerous staff, all, like himself, in the most showy uniforms."[8] Magruder was indeed the guiding light of the thin, brave front along the Warwick River.

Magruder even became so bold to launch sorties across the Warwick against the Union pickets. Brigadier General Cadmus Wilcox on 11 April sent out a strike force from Wynne's Mill that drove the enemy skirmishers back from the river's edge into their entrenchment. The Confederates at Dam No. 1 would often cross the river at night to establish picket posts on the Union side of the dam. Confederate W.H. Andrews remembered wading through the cold water along the dam on the evening of 15 April and reaching close enough to the Union pickets "to hear them whisper." After spending the night in the mud on the riverbank, Andrews recrossed the river just before dawn. When he and his compatriots reached the Confederate earthworks and apparent safety, "the alarm was given." Andrews recounted:

The soldiers to a man, sprung to their feet. Their guns flashed over the works, and for the time being, I thought that I was a dead man. But just in time to save us, someone spoke. The guns were withdrawn from over the works and we ascended safe, but badly scared. It certainly was a close call, and one I don't wish to go through with again.[9]

The Confederate navy continued to harass McClellan and disrupt his desire to move up the York River toward Richmond. On the morning of 11 April, the *Virginia* once again steamed into Hampton Roads accompanied by several gunboats. The Federal fleet scattered out of the harbor into the Chesapeake Bay, and the *Monitor* refused to engage the Confederate ironclad. Fort Wool fired two shots at the *Virginia*, both of which fell short. The *Virginia* then moved into the center of the roadstead, occasionally trading fire with the Union forces. Unfortunately for the Federals, they focused all their attention on the Confederate ironclad, and this enabled the *Jamestown* and *Raleigh* to slip across Hampton Roads to attack Union shipping off Hampton Creek. There, the two Southern steamers were able to capture three Union transports. The Confederate fleet, confident that its show of force had let the Union command realize that Hampton Roads was under its control, steamed back to Craney Island by late afternoon.

The Army of the Potomac seemed destined to have to force its way through the Confederate fortifications without naval support. The army was indeed ready to try. The Northern divisional commanders and their soldiers all sought an opportunity to break the siege and assault that they considered to be a weak Confederate line along the Warwick. Robert Sneden commented about the Union's lack of initiative to strike against Dam No. 1 when he wrote:

> *Our front lines extend four miles from the Warwick Court House to the York River. We have 53,000 men here, of whom 42,000 are with colors and ready for battle. The enemy we know to have 13,000 and every engineer officer as well as others wonder why McClellan doesn't order an immediate assault on the left of our position on Lee's Mill, where the enemy have only a few men to finish their unfinished earthworks.*[10]

The Federals finally did launch one attack on 16 April at Dam No. 1, the midpoint of Magruder's line. This failed Union assault, also referred to as Burnt Chimneys (or, incorrectly, Lee's Mill), was a baptism of fire for many soldiers, like Vermonter Private Wilbur Fisk, who would remember it as a short, vicious fight along "a creek with a wide dam, which drank the blood of many of our men."[11]

Union and Confederate troops had been facing each other across the Warwick at Dam No. 1 since the siege's beginning. The dam was one of three built by Magruder to turn the sluggish stream into a defensive asset. It was located between two prewar tide mills, Lee's Mill and Wynne's Mill. According to Sergeant W.H. Andrews of the 1st Georgia Regulars, the dam had turned the meandering Warwick from twelve to fifteen feet in width to seventy-five to one hundred yards across. The position had been strengthened by a front line of rifle pits near the river's edge backed by two lines of deeper trenches. The first line contained several strong redoubts for artillery, and the second was for the protection of unengaged infantry. The entire position mounted three guns. The dam itself, built at Garrow's Ford, was defended by a one-gun redoubt "occupied by a 12-pounder Napoleon double charged with canister," Sergeant Andrews recorded.[12] This gun was under the command of Captain Jordan. Two other guns, a brass 6-pounder commanded by Lieutenant Alexander Franklin Pope and a brass 12-pounder howitzer commanded by Lieutenant Edward Lumpkin from the Troup Artillery, were positioned in earthworks behind and to the right of the dam. Trees were felled to facilitate Confederate field of fire. The limbs had been thrown into the Warwick River as obstacles to make any attempted river crossing that much more difficult. Unfortunately, the redoubts had been poorly designed—the two supporting guns of the Troup Artillery were positioned too low to effectively shell the Union positions across the river.

The Union and Confederate artilleries at Dam No. 1 often exchanged salvos. Private Henry Beckley of the Hanover Artillery, who was stationed in one of the redoubts defending the dam, noted that each day his battery would commence "firing occasionally at the Yanks."[13] Sergeant Andrews remembered a Federal shell bursting nearby while he and two fellow soldiers were resting against stumps behind the front line at Dam No. 1. All three were hit with shrapnel. Andrews was wounded slightly in his knee, but his two friends were killed instantly. Andrews would never forget Private Boyle and the contrast between his dead countenance and the ambrotype of a smiling young woman in his pocket. "But such is life and such is war," Andrews reflected.[14] "The first thing we knew of them," Lieutenant Robert Miller remembered about the shelling, "is a shrill whistle unlike any thing you or I ever heard before, then the sharp bell-like crack of the bomb—the whistle of little balls like bumble-bees—then the report of the guns."[15] Surprisingly, only three men from Miller's unit, the 14th Louisiana, were wounded by Federal shells during the siege. Dam No. 1 was a dangerous, exposed position that the Confederates continued to strengthen despite the intermittent rifle and artillery fire. "There are about a thousand and one Negroes at work fortifying this place," wrote Private Edmund Dewitt Patterson when holding the rifle pits along the shore. "The Yanks are in plain view, and make us quite careful about having our heads exposed about the breastworks."[16] Some Federal soldiers observed black slaves working on the Confederate fortifications and believed that the Southerners were organizing them into regiments. Lieutenant Charles Harvey Brewster thought that "lots of the enemy's Pickets are negroes probably the chivalry do not like to expose themselves to such dangerous business."[17]

Many Union officers believed the Confederate line could be broken at several weak points along the Warwick River, but McClellan was determined to wait until all his heavy artillery was in place before bombarding Yorktown, only then launching a concerted assault. The outnumbered Southern soldiers' expected attack finally came on 16 April. Since the siege's first day, Baldy Smith had wanted to attack the Confederate line, but McClellan had rejected the thought of any such move, telegraphing Lincoln on 7 April: "The Warwick River grows worse the more you look at it."[18] On 15 April, McClellan reviewed Smith's position at Garrow's Field across from Dam No. 1. The place had been named by the Vermont troops holding the position as Burnt Chimneys for the three stark chimneys that defined the site as the only remaining remnant of the Garrow family farm. The house, Merry Oaks, had been burned by the Confederates (although many Southerners incorrectly blamed the Federals) just before the Union troops approached the Warwick River. The Garrow family had already suffered an even greater loss a few months before when John Toomer Garrow, a private in the Warwick Beauregards, had contracted "camp fever" at Wynne's Mill and died in November 1861. Merry Oaks' charred remnants appeared to be, according to Confederate artillerist Henry Berkley, as "a useless… destruction of private property…but such is war."[19]

McClellan, having observed the continued Confederate defensive preparations, decided to allow Smith's troops to move against the Confederate works at Dam No. 1. He wanted Smith to disrupt the Confederate efforts to strengthen their earthworks, silence their batteries and gain control of the dam. As McClellan left Garrow's Field the evening before the attack, he rode among his troops, telling them, "Goodnight my lads; we will find out what is in front of us and then go at them."[20] The next day, Pennsylvanian Luther Furst observed how McClellan mingled with his soldiers to boost their morale when he wrote in his diary how the Army of the Potomac commander "[t]ook a view of Rebel fortifications…While riding along he stopped and lit his cigar from one of the private's pipes."[21] McClellan's men adored him and had total confidence that he would guide them to victory.

Smith received confirmation of McClellan's intentions at dawn, and Brigadier General William Thomas Harbaugh Brooks's Vermont Brigade (also known as the Green Mountain Boys) immediately began to deploy toward the river. At about 8:00 a.m. on the sixteenth, under cover of artillery fire provided by Captain Thaddeus P. Mott's 3rd New York Battery, Colonel Breed N. Hyde's 3rd Vermont and Colonel Edwin Henry Stoughton's 4th Vermont moved through the woods on both sides of the dam. All six companies of the 3rd Vermont and Companies B and G of the 4th Vermont deployed as skirmishers on the river's edge.

The Confederates were taken somewhat by the "fire of shell upon us," Colonel William Levy of the 2nd Louisiana later reported.[22] The six guns of

A "Dam Failure"

Right: Brigadier General Edwin Stoughton, USA. *Courtesy of the Vermont Historical Society.*

Below: Battle of Dam No. 1, morning. Illustration by Mary Kayaselcuk, Newport News Historical Services Division. *Courtesy of the Virginia War Museum.*

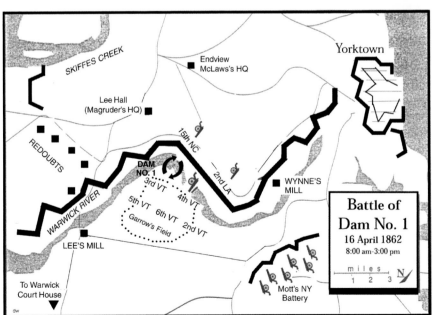

Mott's Battery dueled with the three Confederate guns positioned near the dam. Confederate rifle fire slackened, but the artillery counter-fire proved effective. The first shell fired by the Confederates disabled one of Mott's guns, killing three gunners and wounding several more. The 12-pounder in the redoubt defending the dam had been disabled and replaced by a 6-pounder from the Troup Artillery under the command of Lieutenant Pope. The old artillerist Magruder praised Lieutenant Pope's handling of his gun, which "was served with the greatest accuracy and effect and by the coolness and skill with which it was handled the greatest odds against us were almost completely counter balanced."[23] Yet the Union cannon fire soon began to have a telling effect on its Confederate counterparts. After three hours of artillery and rifle fire, the Southerners appeared to have abandoned their one-gun battery.

Now Smith began a personal reconnaissance of the Confederate positions. The Union artillery fire and Vermont skirmishers were successful in halting work on the Southern entrenchments and had silenced their battery, achieving McClellan's initial goal for this action. Smith reported that "the gun in the angle of the upper work had been replaced by a wooden gun, and that scarcely anybody showed above the parapet, the skirmishers from the 4th Vermont doing good execution."[24] Lieutenant Edwin M. Noyes, aide to General Brooks, then crossed the waist-deep river below the dam and approached within fifty yards of the Confederate works undiscovered. The Federals realized that the Southern position at Dam No. 1 was extremely weak and could perhaps be carried with an assault.

McClellan arrived on the scene at noon, accompanied by his royal French aides, the Prince de Joinville and the Comte de Paris. Upon hearing Noyes's report and grasping the possibility of carrying the Confederate works, thereby splitting the Warwick Line in two, he ordered Baldy Smith to bring up his entire division. McClellan qualified the command by advising Smith to avoid a general engagement if serious resistance was encountered.

Smith reinforced his position with Captain Romeyn B. Ayres's Battery F, 5th U.S. Artillery, and Captain Charles C. Wheeler's Battery E, 1st New York, and planned to use units from the 3rd Vermont Regiment to test the Confederate positions across the river. If the Vermonters were successful in driving the enemy out of their rifle pits, they were to cheer and wave a white handkerchief and more troops would be sent across the Warwick. Smith also ordered the rest of his division, two brigades under the command of Winfield Scott Hancock and John W. Davidson, to be ready to exploit any success achieved by the Vermonters.

A "Dam Failure"

Battle of Dam No. 1, 16 April 1862. *Courtesy of the Vermont Historical Society.*

Following an apparently effective Federal cannonade, Smith sent four companies of the 3rd Vermont across the river to capture the Confederate rifle pits below the dam. These men were under the command of Captain Fernando C. Harrington. They crossed the Warwick under heavy fire and captured the enemy's position along the water's edge. It had been a difficult passage. The Vermonters had to carry their muskets and cartridge boxes over their heads while contending with a muddy, root-filled river bottom and trees felled by the Confederates to serve as obstacles. Eventually, most of the 192 men who entered the shoulder-deep water—the wounded being dragged by coat, collar or arm—made it to the other side and gave a great cheer as they chased the Southerners out of their entrenchments.

Surprised by the Vermonter's bold rush and confused by an unauthorized order, the 15th North Carolina fell back in a panic that one Vermonter, Erastus Buck, thought made them "look like a flock of sheep."[25] It was the North Carolinians' first day in the trenches at Dam No. 1. The unit had just returned to Magruder's command after brief duty near Goldsboro, North Carolina, and it was their first engagement. The Carolinians fell back behind a redoubt, where the commander of the 15th, 1856 VMI graduate Colonel Robert M. McKinney, tried to rally and reform his men. McKinney was killed instantly by a ball through the forehead as he readied his men for a counterattack. The 15th then huddled behind a redoubt, and the entire Confederate line at Dam No. 1 was in disarray.

The Green Mountain Boys were also in a dangerous position. Most of their ammunition was wet and useless. Expected reinforcements never materialized. Captain Alonzo Hutchinson, who had been entrusted with Brooks's handkerchief to give the signal for reinforcements, lay mortally wounded on the banks of the Warwick. At this moment, Baldy Smith had taken his second fall from his horse and was somewhat senseless. Leadership among the Vermonters had fallen on the shoulders of Captain Samuel E. Pingree of Company F, as Harrington seemed to have faded away from action. Pingree, however, was seriously wounded, his thumb shot off, and he was bleeding profusely from a wound in his hip.

Meanwhile, the Confederate lines were stirring like a hornets' nest. The eminent Brigadier General Howell Cobb—a former governor of Georgia, secretary of treasury under President Buchanan, ex-speaker of the U.S. House of Representatives and speaker of the Confederate Provisional Congress—was a dynamic motivator of men and the commander of Cobb's Brigade. He reinforced the 15th North Carolina with the 7th, 8th, 11th and 16th Georgia Regiments and the 2nd Louisiana. Cobb reorganized the Confederate troops, "riding in among the men," according to Lafayette McLaws, and "they recognized his voice and his person, and promptly retook their positions."[26] The 7th Georgia led the Confederate counterattack amid "the greatest applause and golléring,"[27] Georgian Eli Pinson Landers recounted to his mother after the battle. The Vermonters, however, were slow to give up their toehold on the Confederate side

Top: Captain Samuel Pingree, USA. *Courtesy of the Vermont Historical Society.*

Bottom: Brigadier General Howell Cobb, CSA. *Courtesy of the University of Georgia Library.*

of the Warwick despite the mounting pressure from Cobb's troops and regiments commanded by Colonel George Thomas "Tige" Anderson. An order was given to retreat back across the river, and it was organized by Lieutenant Robert D. Whittemore of Company E since Pingree was faint from loss of blood. Some soldiers did not hear the command and were slow to respond. Others, like Erastus Buck, felt that "a retreat was almost sure destruction" and attempted "to make the last and desperate charge."[28] These few men could not stem the Confederate advance and fell back across the Warwick. Regaining their rifle pits, the resurgent Rebels continued their fire and, according to Lieutenant Buck, made the water "boil with their bullets."[29]

The Union troops had held the Confederate trenches for almost forty minutes and suffered a majority of their casualties while recrossing the "fatal stream." Musician Julian Scott described the gunfire to a *New York Tribune* reporter as being "just like sap-boiling, in the stream, the bullets fell so thick."[30] It had been a vicious little fight. Private Landers of Cobb's Legion described "the Truth" about the Confederate counterattack:

> *We did not have time to organize our regiment. We all run in and shot when we had the chance and never formed no line. If a man could get behind a tree it was alright. Some of the boys never fired a gun. Some lay behind logs as close to the ground as young rabbits till the battle was over. One or two of our company run back to camp but as for my part I thought I would stay till the fun was over…It did not frighten me as bad as I expected it would but I tell you when the bullets would whistle around my head I felt sort of ticklish.*[31]

Brigadier General Lafayette McLaws quickly brought his entire division into the vicinity of Dam No. 1 to halt any possible breakthrough. Baldy Smith, now back on his horse and apparently lucid, decided to try the Confederate lines once again with another piecemeal attack. At 5:00 p.m., following a Federal cannonade from twenty-three guns, Smith sent units from Stoughton's 4th Vermont to cross above the dam to capture the one-gun battery and troops from Colonel Nathan Lord's 6th Vermont below the dam to recapture the Confederate rifle pits. Neither attack was successful due to heavy fire from the Confederate entrenchments. By dark, the Battle of Dam No. 1 was over, with 165 Federal and 90 Confederate casualties. Magruder, who was at Dam No. 1 during part of the engagement, left the tactical management to Lafayette McLaws. In his report about the battle,

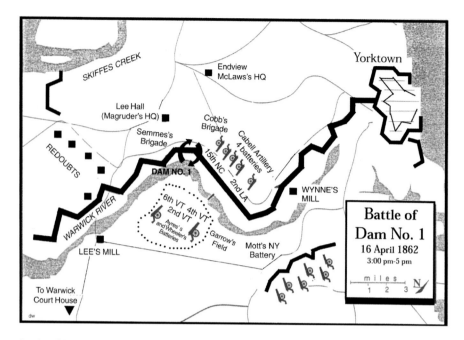

Battle of Dam No.1, afternoon. Illustration by Mary Kayaselcuk, Newport News Historical Services Division. *Courtesy of the Virginia War Museum.*

Magruder praised McLaws, noting that, "[t]he dispositions of General McLaws were skillfully made. His whole being and conduct is deserving of the highest commendation."[32]

The attack against Dam No. 1, the weakest section of the Confederate defenses, failed because the Federals were unwilling to rapidly commit additional troops to support the Vermonters' initial assault. General Smith reflected after the battle that among the men of the 3rd Vermont who crossed the river, there were "more individual acts of heroism performed than he had ever heard of."[33] The Confederates even referred to the Vermonters as "brave rascals." Two Medals of Honor were awarded for gallantry on 16 April. Captain Samuel E. Pingree, later governor of Vermont, received his in 1891 for bravery during the engagement. The other was presented to Julian Scott in February 1865. The sixteen-year-old Scott crossed the river at least two times following the first assault, saving "no less than nine of his comrades." One of these men was the mortally wounded Private William Scott. Scott was known as the "sleeping sentinel" and had been pardoned by President Lincoln in late 1861 from a firing squad. His reprieve had led him to say, "I will show President Lincoln that I am not afraid to die for my country."[34] Scott fulfilled his pledge at Dam No. 1.

The battle was the Vermont Brigade's first engagement, and the Vermonters' conduct was "worthy of veterans," McClellan later noted in his report about the engagement. Corporal George Q. French wrote to his friends at home about the battle, "The 3rd Vermont has won a name, but Oh!, at what a cost."[35] The dead and wounded Vermonters lay where they were shot for the next two days. Finally, Colonel Levy of the 2nd Louisiana crossed Dam No. 1 under a flag of truce to arrange for their burial. During the truce, Levy asked what unit forced the 15th North Carolina's retreat. When he was told it was just a detachment of the 3rd Vermont, he exclaimed that it "was lucky for us that you did not send over many such detachments."[36]

There were also numerous recriminations after the battle, as many thought, like Corporal French, that "a glorious victory might have been gained."[37] Harrington was accused of not providing effective leadership (some soldiers said that he never crossed the Warwick) and was later discharged by "special order of the War Department" on 23 July 1862. The blame for the failure to break Magruder's line at Dam No. 1 fell on Baldy Smith,

Top: Private William Scott, 3rd Vermont Regiment. *Courtesy of the Vermont Historical Society.*

Bottom: Musician Julian Scott, 3rd Vermont Regiment. *Courtesy of the Vermont Historical Society.*

Graves of 3rd Vermont Volunteers killed at Dam No. 1. *Courtesy of the Vermont Historical Society.*

whom some accused of being drunk on the battlefield. His two falls off his horse did not strengthen his case, but he was later exonerated by his corps commander, General Keyes, who was at Dam No. 1 during the engagement. Others blamed no one but simply declared the attack a "[d]am failure."[38] Even though several other skilled officers were on hand observing the assault, including 1841 West Point graduate W.T.H. Brooks and 1859 West Point graduate Edwin Stoughton, they did not seize the initiative to organize a relief attack to support the Vermonters stranded on the other side of the Warwick River. Brooks later lamented that his troops had found themselves "in something we did not exactly finish."[39] Smith concluded that the attack was not pressed because of orders from McClellan (who also witnessed the battle) not to bring on a major engagement, stating, "Thus a fair opportunity to break the Warwick line was missed."[40]

Siege

C onfederate artillerist Corporal J.W. Minnish called the Union attack at Dam No. 1 simply "ten days too late."[1] McClellan, however, wrote to Secretary of War Edwin Stanton that his army had made good progress on 16 April along the Warwick, to which Stanton replied, "Good for the first lick! Hurrah for Smith and the one-gun battery. Let us have Yorktown with Magruder and his gang before the first of May and the job will be over."[2]

McClellan had no intention of pressing forward despite Stanton's urging and quickly dismissed the engagement from his mind. Goldsborough's squadron in Hampton Roads was reinforced by the ironclad USS *Galena.* The arrival of this six-gun ironclad enabled the flag officer to increase the security of McClellan's transports and to better contain the Confederate ironclad. Meanwhile, McClellan concentrated on building batteries for his heavy guns and parallel trenches necessary to unleash his grand bombardment; he knew this would force the Confederate evacuation of the Warwick-Yorktown Line.

The siege was to last another two weeks. While McClellan worked on his preparations, General Joseph E. Johnston continued reinforcing Magruder's army. Johnston finally came to the Peninsula in the second week of April to take command of the combined force, which would eventually number fifty-six thousand men. Even though he lauded Magruder's "delaying tactics," he was dismayed by what he found on the Peninsula. After he inspected Magruder's defenses on 12 April, Johnston returned to Richmond and advised President Davis that he could not hold the Warwick-Yorktown Line. "Labor enough has been expended here to make a very strong position," the commanding general wrote, "but it has been wretchedly misapplied by the young engineer officers. No one but McClellan could have hesitated to attack. The fight for Yorktown must be one of artillery, in which we cannot win. The result is certain; the time only doubtful."[3]

Robert E. Lee and Secretary of War George W. Randolph (who had fought at Big Bethel under Magruder's command) counseled that the Warwick-Yorktown Line should be held as long as possible because a retreat from the Peninsula would mean the loss of Norfolk. With Norfolk gone, the CSS *Virginia* would be without a port, and her crew would have to destroy her, thereby opening the James River to the Federal navy. Furthermore, Lee wanted time for the Confederate army so that it could be reorganized from a volunteer to conscripted force. Johnston attended the meeting with his two "wing commanders," James Longstreet and G.W. Smith. Neither was very supportive as Smith was ill and Longstreet could not hear well. Johnston countered Lee's proposal with two concepts of his own. He pressed for the unification of all Confederate armies (Magruder's and Huger's commands to be added to Johnston's Army of the Potomac) and to fight the final battle for the Confederate capital outside of Richmond. He also suggested that his army should strike at Washington and leave Magruder's command at Yorktown. This action, Johnston believed, would surely force McClellan to fall back to defend Washington. Davis considered all the arguments and ordered Johnston to hold the line of the Peninsula. Johnston truly believed the capital should be defended on the outskirts of Richmond and never intended to totally comply with President Davis's command to hold the Warwick-Yorktown Line. He later wrote, "The belief that events on the Peninsula would soon compel the Confederate government to adopt my method of opposing the Federal army, reconciled me somewhat to the necessity of obeying the President's order."[4]

The siege dragged on despite Johnston's protestations, and with it the soldiers suffered from exposure and enemy fire. Lieutenant Robert M. Miller of the Concordia Rifles wrote his mother from Wynne's Mill to say that he and his men "have dug Rifle pits and are compelled to eat, sleep and stand in them from day to night and night to day."[5] The soldiers continually complained about standing or sitting in trenches "with water up to our knees," as Sergeant W.H. Andrews of the 1st Georgia Regulars remembered of his service at Dam No. 1.[6] A member of the Richmond Howitzers, Richard Channing Price, thought that he had "gotten along very well without my boots, though I should have liked to have them in this wet weather."[7] "During the month of April," Jubal Early later wrote, "there was much cold, rainy weather, and our troops suffered greatly, as they were without tents or other shelter."[8] Private Patterson could only agree when he wrote in his diary that there was "rain and mud in abundance, and the only articles, except sickness that we have a sufficiency of."[9] Captain Vines Edmunds Turner, then a lieutenant in the 23rd North Carolina, recalled:

The trenches themselves filled with water and could not be drained. Yet the artillery and rifle fire of the enemy held the men close down in them. No fire could be kindled day or night without its becoming the focus of heavy shell fire and it was therefore strictly forbidden. The only food was flour and salt meat and these in diminishing quantities. Food was cooked by details in the rear and brought forward to us. Men sickened by the thousands. Soldiers actually died in the mud and water of the trenches before they could be taken to the hospital. And many of the cases of illness were measles. This exposure meant death. Thus unavoidably died a dog's death many a gallant fellow.[10]

"In addition to all this," Jubal Early commented later about the soldiers' living conditions along the Warwick, "their rations were very limited and consisted of the plainest and roughest food...All this told terribly on the health of his men, and there was little or no hospital accommodations in the rear."[11] James B. Griffin of Hampton's Legion agreed with Early's assessment as he wrote his wife, "The living here is pretty tight. We get nothing but bread and meat, and occasionally coffee—Mostly Sassafras Tea. Butter and milk is unknown."[12] The Confederates did not allow fires along the front lines, and as more of Johnston's troops arrived, they overtaxed Magruder's supply system. Food, or the lack thereof, was a problem for both armies. McClellan's army required sixty tons of supplies each day, and this caused the Union soldiers to forage the countryside to augment their meager army rations. Pennsylvanian Oliver W. Norton justified such appropriations because any food found on a local farm "is nothing else but secesh, and when Uncle Sam can't furnish food, I see nothing wrong in requiring it of our enemies."[13] Lieutenant Charles Brewster of the 10th Massachusetts wrote his mother, "The inhabitants here have fled leaving everything and the woods are full of cattle, horses and hogs. Our boys have been bringing in quarters of beef all day long. They build up a fire hang up the beef on a stake and soon are revelling in roast beef, or beef steaks, or pork or mutton."[14] Such feasts were savored by the soldiers and were not uncommon. Often the soldiers sought refuge in a good meal once they were relieved from frontline duty. Alabamian Edmund Dewitt Patterson wrote:

> *Our mess were gathered around a camp kettle filled with "peasoup" up in one of the cabins that had been built by the 2nd Fla. for winter quarters—each with a spoon, and all eating out of the kettle and enjoying it hugely—when all at once a shell burst over our house, and we thought perhaps that there was going to be a general attack, but heard nothing more for about half a minute. Then a shell came through our little cabin, cutting a log out of each side of it, passing over our heads, and ruining our soup with mud and splinters. It was just as well that it did for we all lost our appetites.*[15]

The food and weather may have been generally miserable, but the soldiers had an even greater fear of the daily and intermittent, yet constant, rifle and cannon fire. "There is more or less skirmishing every day between the Pickets," South Carolinian James Griffin wrote. "Occasionally a man struck but not often."[16] It was still dangerous work, as a Sergeant Andrews noted that "it was worth a man's life to show his head above the works."[17]

Wynne's Mill earthworks overlooking the Warwick River. *Courtesy of John Moran Quarstein.*

Colonel Hiram Berdan, USA. *Courtesy of the U.S. Army Military Historical Institute.*

Vines Edmunds Turner recalled the day when his unit first entered the frontline defenses along the Warwick River and the sensation felt by all the soldiers when the first shell burst among them when he wrote that one tongue-tied warrior exclaimed, "Dam 'fi come here to be hulled out this way when I can't see who's shootin' at me."[18] New Jersey Private Alfred Bellard observed one soldier "more venturesome than the rest, mounted the magizine [*sic*] of the fort in plain sight of the rebels. In a moment the shells were flying around lively."[19] "Many a poor Yankee has fallen in view of us," wrote Confederate Robert E. Lewis with glee at Lee's Mill. "How the devils squall when they were shot and how strange it may seem I rejoyced at it. The whiz of shells and bullets sound as natural as the bark of a dog."[20] One night, members of Birney's Zouaves were on picket duty at Lee's Mill when unit members watched a Confederate officer swinging a lantern walk down to the river. When Private John McGraw prepared to shoot him, another soldier, William Albertson, grasped his rifle, saying, "Don't fire, Jack; it looks like murder to shoot him."[21]

The Union army deployed companies from Berdan's Sharpshooters at various locations up and down the twelve-mile line. The 1st U.S. Sharpshooters, generally called Berdan's Sharpshooters, was organized by the top marksman in the United States, Colonel Hiram Berdan. He and his men wore green uniforms to help disguise themselves as they hid in treetops or among the shrubbery. These sharpshooters, according to Private Bellard, "were always on the look out for game, and woe to the rebel who put himself in their way."[22] "These sharpshooters are the greatest terror to the enemy," wrote Charles Brewster, "and well they may be for no sooner does one of them Rebels show himself then plunk goes a bullet into his body, and he is done from secession for this world."[23] David Ritchie of the 1st New York Light Artillery agreed with Brewster, noting, "Our sharpshooters have become a terror to the enemy, though this lying in wait and picking off men singly is after all a barbarous method of warfare and has little to do with shortening the rebellion."[24] At Dam No. 1, also called Garrow's Chimney, George Armstrong Custer wrote that he supervised the construction of a rifle pit for Berdan's men that was close enough to the Confederate lines that "the voices of the enemy could be distinctly heard while engaged in ordinary conversation" and from which the "sharpshooters took particular delight…as it afforded them a fine opportunity to exercise their peculiar accomplishment."[25] Either hidden in rifle pits or concealed in treetop positions, the sharpshooters added fierceness to the siege, as Confederate artillerist Major Robert Stiles wrote, "The Federal sharpshooters were as audacious and deadly as I ever saw them." Stiles considered them "a fearful thing. The regular sharpshooter often seems to me little better than a human tiger lying in wait for blood."[26] "As the sharpshooting grew hotter," Vines Edmunds Turner remembered, "the pickets could only be posted and relieved at night."[27]

It was difficult for the Confederates to respond to this Union marksmanship, as Jubal Early commented, "Our whole armament for the infantry consisted of smooth-bore muskets, and our artillery ammunition was too scarce to permit its use in contrast with sharpshooters." The lines were so close and the rifle fire so deadly at Dam No. 1 and Wynne's Mill that "it had been necessary to cut zig-zag trenches, or bayous, to enable the men to pass into and from the works with as little exposure as possible," Early added.[28] "It was much as a man's life was worth even peep over the top parapet," Corporal J.W. Minnish remembered when he visited the Confederate trenches at Dam No. 1 after the 16 April engagement. Minnish witnessed the skill of Northern marksmanship when one soldier placed his hat on a stick and held it above the parapet for a brief moment and then withdrew it. Upon examination, Minnish found "the crown neatly perforated by an enemy's bullet." Southerners struck back as Minnish watched "Big Bill" Griffith from the 1st Kentucky slowly take aim at puffs of smoke from a tall pine tree. Soon the Union sharpshooter "tumbled down into the dam with a loud splash. That ended that."[29]

The siege also had its informal truces between the opposing forces witnessing varying levels of bantering and some relief from the shot and shell. Sergeant George B. Noyles of the 11th Maine Volunteers was amazed that the Lee's Mill area was such "a place of desecration and desolation" but also advised his father that "[o]n the opposite side of the river we can observe the rebel batteries. The Johnnies on picket are quite friendly. We lay down our arms, meet between the lines, and hold conversation, ect. for a few minutes, then return respectfully to our lines."[30] James Rush Holmes of the 61st Pennsylvania wrote his aunt, "As they have only a large room together, they throwing up a Bull Run to our boys and we Fort Donaldson and other places."[31] Such lapses of aggression were usually temporary, yet they reinforced the ironic futility of this War Between the States. "It is not odd to think," Brigadier General Philip Kearny wrote his wife, "that Magruder, one of my best friends, is one of the chief men here. This is a most unnatural war."[32] Lafayette McLaws also wrote his wife about his many friends and acquaintances who were serving in leadership roles in the Union army. "On the other side we hear of Gen. Brooks who is an old friend of mine," McLaws recounted. "Gen. Davidson, an acquaintance of mine & General W.S. Smith, who was a particular of many of the officers here, & lastly, Gen. McClellan was a friend of mine."[33] Besides these thoughts and briefly formed friendships, most of the soldiers simply wished the siege to end, as Lieutenant Robert Miller expressed to his mother: "The April sunshine changed to rain, and the heavens have been weeping bitter cold tears ever since perhaps for the prospect of blasted human happiness that is so soon to follow."[34]

The siege's monotony was occasionally broken by the sight of balloons floating over the lines. Professor Thaddeus S.C. Lowe had commanded the U.S. Army Balloon Corps since August 1861. He operated his heavily varnished harvest-moon orange balloons using a mobile hydrogen gas generator. Lowe had brought two balloons, the *Intrepid* and the *Constitution*, to the Peninsula on his balloon barge, the *George Washington Park Custis*. The balloons were typically operated using three to four tether ropes and two men, an operator and an observer, who would go aloft in a wicker basket dressed with star bunting. The *Intrepid* was based at Yorktown. Flights became a familiar sight, with Fitz-John Porter taking several trips above the lines. On the morning of 10 April, Porter went up in the balloon alone. He had wished to achieve a higher elevation, so only one tether rope was used. Unfortunately, just as the operator, James Allen, prepared to get into the basket, the rope broke with a loud snap, like the sound of a gunshot, and up went the *Intrepid*, out of control. Porter, who had observed how to operate the balloon, remained calm. As the balloon floated over Confederate lines, he took notes, and when it drifted back over Union lines, he was able to land it safely. McClellan wrote his wife about the incident:

I am just recovering from a terrible scare. Early this morning I was awakened by a dispatch...stating that Fitz had made an ascension in the balloon & and that the balloon had broken away & had come to ground some 3 miles SW—which would be within the enemy's lines! You can imagine how I felt! I at once sent off various pickets to find out what they knew & try to do something to save him—but the order had no sooner gone, than in walks Mr. Fitz just as cool as casual—he had luckily come down near my own camp after actually passing over that of the enemy!!

You may rest assured of one thing: you won't catch me in the confounded balloon nor will I allow any other Generals to go up in it![35]

Porter and Barnard continued to make use of balloon observations to aid their locating Union siege guns. A second balloon camp for the *Constitution* was established at Warwick Court House on 10 April. George Armstrong Custer enjoyed the dubious honor of making several ascents in this balloon to observe the Confederate defenses between Lee's Mill and Dam No. 1. At first, Custer "ridiculed the system of balloon reconnaissance"[36] when he was ordered to go up in the *Constitution* with Lowe's assistant, John Allen. As a cavalryman, Custer thought, "I had a choice as to the character of the mount, but the proposed ride was far more elevated than I had ever desired or contemplated."[37] When asked by Allen if he wished to go up in the balloon alone, Custer replied that his desire, "if frankly expressed, would not have been to go up at all."[38] Custer was nervous about the basket construction, and as the balloon rose into the sky, the young lieutenant noted, "I was urged to stand up also. My confidence in balloons at that time was not sufficient, however, to justify such a course, so I remained in the bottom of the basket, with a firm hold on either side."[39] Once the *Constitution* reached the proper altitude, Custer was able to overcome his fears and stood up to make observations. He recounted:

To the right could be seen the York River, following which the eye could rest on Chesapeake Bay. On the left, and at about the same distance, flowed the James River…Between these two rivers extended a most beautiful landscape, and no less interesting than beautiful.[40]

He was able to record the Confederate positions located below him:

The point over which the balloon was held was probably one mile from the nearest point of the enemy's line. In an open country balloons would be invaluable in discovering the location of the enemy's camps and works.

…The enemy's camps, like our own, were generally pitched in the woods… his earthworks along the Warwick were also concealed by growing timber…

Right: Brigadier General Fitz-John Porter, USA. *Courtesy of the Library of Congress.*

Below: Balloon *Constitution. Courtesy of John Moran Quarstein.*

Here and there the dim outline of an earthwork could be seen more than half concealed by the trees which gave been purposely left standing on their front. Guns can be seen mounted and peering sullenly through the embrasures, while men in considerable numbers were standing in and around entrenchments, often collected in groups, intently observing the balloon, curious, no doubt, to know the character or value of the information its occupants could derive from their elevated post of observation.[41]

Though Custer took several flights, he could never accurately estimate the number of Confederates defending to prove or disprove Allan Pinkerton's reports of more than 100,000 soldiers supporting the Warwick-Yorktown defenses. Pinkerton, who gained a grand reputation of prewar detective work, set up the Secret Service after the First Battle of Manassas. Using contrabands and deserters, he presented McClellan with high evaluation of Confederate troop strength that only supported the Union general's belief, based on his scholarship about sieges, that Magruder would have only defended the Warwick-Yorktown Line if he had at least 10,000 men per mile. Nevertheless, Lowe's balloons were extremely helpful as the Federal officers developed their siege works and built batteries to eventually bombard Yorktown.

The Confederates responded, not only with artillery (cannons elevated by Edward Porter Alexander to serve as antiaircraft guns) but also with their own balloon. It was a roughly made hot air device, rather than Lowe's gas type, commanded by one of Magruder's aides, John Randolph Bryan of Gloucester County. Actually, Bryan had volunteered for a special assignment and was surprised to learn from General Johnston at his temporary Lee Hall headquarters that flying in a balloon was his reconnaissance duty. Bryan protested at first, noting, "I had never even seen a balloon, and I knew absolutely nothing about the management of it." As the balloon rose up above the treetops, Bryan remembered how the Federal shells and bullets "whistled and sang...a most unpleasant music"[42] around him. "Yesterday the rebels sent up a balloon directly in front of us," New York artillerist David Ritchie commented, from Warwick Court House, "but it was it was not in the air more than five minutes when it suddenly descended much faster than it rose, having received a sharpshooter's bullet."[43]

The Confederate balloon was never struck by enemy fire, however, and Bryan made several flights from Lee Hall (then known as Lee's Farm), Wynne's Mill and Yorktown to observe Federal siege preparations. Even though Bryan made his subsequent aerial observations "with somewhat less trepidation," the young aeronaut's last voyage almost resulted in disaster when a severed tether rope sent him off on a free flight. Bryan remembered how "the balloon jerked upward as if by some great force for about two miles, or so it seemed to me. I was breathless and gasping, and trembling like a leaf from fear without knowing what had happened beyond the surmise that the rope which held me to the earth had broken." The Confederate aeronaut was blown over the camp of the 2nd Florida Regiment. The Confederates mistook Bryan's balloon for a Federal spy device and began shooting at him. The balloon then drifted over the York River and "began to settle quite rapidly," Bryan recalled. "It was evident that I would be dumped in the middle of this broad expanse of water." Bryan stripped off his clothing and boots, preparing for a swim. He could hear the tether line on the water when another breeze blew the balloon back over the banks of the York River and he landed near an apple orchard. It was Bryan's last flight.[44]

Another form of amusement and interest for Federal troops was the deployment of "coffee mill guns" at Warwick Court House. The Agar Gun, invented by Wilson Agar, was a hopper-fed weapon fired by turning a hand

Union Battery No. 1, Yorktown. *Courtesy of the U.S. Army Military Historical Institute.*

crank.[45] Several of those rapid-fire guns were assigned to the 56th New York Volunteers and were brought into service below Lee's Mill. While stationed near the courthouse, Private Patrick Lyons of the 2nd Rhode Island witnessed an Agar Gun "go to the front; this kind of gun is capable of being fired very rapidly which gives it the name of the Corn Sheller and is very destructive against a body of infantry."[46] The Confederates took no notice of this new weapon. Other than instilling some confidence in the Federal troops, neither these rapid-fire guns nor the balloons had any impact on the siege.

Warwick Court House was full of activity during the entire siege. General Keyes had established the IV Corps' headquarters as it was just two miles from the Confederate positions at Lee's Mill. David Ritchie remembered the headquarters site when he wrote:

> *A few rods from us is Warwick Court House, a relic of colonial power and magnificence. It is built of old, imported brick and in magnitude and style much resembles a country schoolhouse. Close by is the county jail and the county clerk's office. In the latter have been found many curious old documents, some of them bearing dates as early as 1670. Before a guard was put over the building, the soldiers had appropriated large quantities of documents, deeds, wills, bonds, testaments, orders, etc. One man gave me part of the last will and testament of one Richard Hill, who flourished and died in 1679. All of the witnesses' names were signed with an "X" mark. I also saw a sheriff's writ of attachment made in the name of His Majesty George III. It is a pity such havoc has been wrought.*[47]

The siege had a tremendous impact on civilian property. Charles Harvey Brewster also reflected on the destruction when he wrote:

> *We took up the line of march of the road past Warwick Court House, which is about half as big as our barn and built of brick. As we passed the open door we could see a safe broken open and any quantity of papers strewed about. The village consists of a store, Tavern, Ct. House, Jail, and one of two houses…There was an old house in the village, and in 15 minutes there was not a board left on it, neither roof, floor nor anything. One of our boys received enough for himself and the three officers, and we made a floor and down we laid, and were soon fast asleep.*[48]

"Whatever may be the crime of the inhabitants it is not right for individuals, whether officers of privates, to judge and punish them," Colonel Charles S.

Warwick Court House, Virginia. *Courtesy of The Mariners' Museum.*

Wainwright of the 1ˢᵗ New York Artillery reflected. "The inhabitants [are] our fellow citizens though they are rebels. Our object is to put down the rebellion, not to widen the breach of estrangement, or to impoverish our own country."[49] Indeed, destruction and despair were everywhere as more than 170,000 soldiers gathered in the siege along the Warwick River.

Johnston returned to the Peninsula following his daylong conference with President Davis on 17 April. He brought with him G.W. Smith's and James Longstreet's divisions, which would bring his army's total strength on the Peninsula to fifty-six thousand. It was almost half the number of McClellan's army. Johnston reorganized the command structure, giving D.H. Hill command of the Yorktown-Gloucester defenses, Longstreet the Confederate center and Magruder the right wing from Dam No. 1 to Mulberry Island. G.W. Smith's command was held in reserve below Williamsburg near the Half-Way House. This reorganization resulted in Magruder's virtual demotion from the commander of the Army of the Peninsula to a divisional commander. Three other generals now outranked him on the Peninsula. This was particularly irksome to Prince John, as many had thought that he might be given command of all the Confederate troops now coming back to the Peninsula. No longer the lead actor, Magruder began to sulk in his headquarters at Lee Hall, criticizing the design and armament of the very defenses he had developed.

Magruder made no outward complaint and sent his army an address lauding Johnston and noting that "by the new arrangements which the exigencies of the service require the late major general commanding finds himself separated from a portion of the old Army of the Peninsula."[50] Lafayette McLaws noted the change in leadership and wrote his wife:

> *The designs of the enemy are wrapped in mystery, as are the designs of our Commander in Chief General Johnston, who is a very quiet, stern man, telling his plans to me.*
>
> *There is a great contrast between the two commanders, General Magruder & General Johnston.*
>
> *General Magruder is fond of dress and parade and of company. Conceals nothing, and delights to have a crowd about him, to whom he converses freely upon any and all subjects. He never moves from his headquarters without having five or six aides & a dozen or more orderlies.*
>
> *General Johnston will never speak on official matters to but the person interested, dislikes to have a crowd about him, never mentions military matters when away from his office. Often rides off alone, never will have more than two men with him. Has not much to say to even his best friends, and does not appear to care about dress, although he always dresses neatly & in a uniform coat—if you have business with him it is yes or no, without talking more than to a proper understanding of the subject.*[51]

McLaws believed that only his West Point classmate, G.W. Smith, had any influence over Joe Johnston.

Besides Magruder, who had already achieved great fame for his exploits on the Peninsula, Joe Johnston's senior officers were noted for their skill and promise. Major General Daniel Harvey Hill, who had served under Magruder during the Battle of Big Bethel, was in command of the Yorktown and Gloucester Point defenses. The most senior of Johnston's divisional commanders was Major General Gustavus Woodson Smith, an 1842 West Point graduate. He had served as an engineer in Mexico and taught engineering at West Point before and after the Mexican War; however, he resigned in 1854 and eventually was named in 1858 New York City's street commissioner. A Kentuckian, Smith suffered a nervous paralysis in summer 1861, and when he went to Hot Springs, Georgia, for a cure, he was considered a disloyal person. Consequently, he offered his services to the Confederacy and was immediately named a major general. G.W. Smith was a big, tall man and a close friend of Joe Johnston. Despite his outward air of confidence, he had never before commanded troops in battle, and the strain of command appeared to affect his well-being. Smith's division was Johnston's reserve and was kept near Williamsburg as the siege reached toward its conclusion. Major General James Longstreet commanded the Confederate center, including the key positions of Wynne's Mill, Red Redoubt and Fort Magruder. Longstreet, known as "Pete," was an 1842 West Point graduate who served with distinction during the Mexican War. From Alabama, Longstreet had been a paymaster before resigning his commission to join the Confederacy. A powerful figure almost six feet in height, broad shouldered and with a heavy beard that almost concealed his mouth, Longstreet had fought at the First Battle of Manassas and had been promoted major general in October 1861. Magruder's new duties as commander of the Confederate right wing gave Prince John leadership of the troops from Mulberry Island to Dam No. 1.

Even before his demotion to right wing commander, Magruder had begun the reorganization of his James River flank. It now became one of his primary concerns. On 14 April, he had ordered his troops to abandon the Minor's Farm Line on Mulberry Island and had several new redoubts built between Skiffes Creek and Lee's Mill to defend access to the Mulberry Island Road. This action provided Prince John with additional troops to fill the Warwick Line trenches between Lee's Mill and Dam No. 1; however, it left Fort Crafford and the water battery on Mulberry Island Point open to attack by a possible Union crossing of the Warwick River. Magruder had decided "to leave the Fort to its fate,"[52] yet the defense of Mulberry Island still troubled him. Even though the *Virginia* denied the Federal navy access to the mouth of the James River, Magruder requested that gunboats be assigned off Mulberry Island as they would be of "immense importance to prevent the enemy from crossing the Warwick and operating on James River."[53] By 21 April, the *Jamestown, Teaser, Raleigh, Patrick Henry* and *Beaufort* were stationed off Mulberry Island and occasionally shelled the Union lines.[54] Magruder's troop dispositions were reported to Johnston on 24 April:

> *Many forces now occupy, in a strictly defensive attitude, the Warwick Line, with the exception that that portion of the Warwick River intervening between Lee's Mill and Minor's Farm, which was originally within our lines, has been abandoned as against any serious demonstration of the*

enemy…the abandonment of the lower portion of the line on Warwick River, influenced doubtless in this determination by a belief in the strength and formidable character of the works at Mulberry Island Point, sufficient in this belief with the aid of the Virginia, to maintain itself alone and unsupported except on the water side by our steamers against any efforts of the enemy.[55]

The entire Confederate army was also going through the throes of unit reorganization due to the passage of the Conscription Act on the same day as the Dam No. 1 engagement. One of Robert E. Lee's reasons for pressing Johnston to hold the line on the Peninsula was to give the army time to complete this transformation from one-year volunteers to soldiers serving for the war's duration. Conscription was not popular with the troops. Private Jesse Reid of the 4th South Carolina, who camped behind the lines in Warwick County, noted that the troops talked of nothing but the Conscription Act, and he was not alone in opposition. In one letter to his family, Reid acknowledged that conscription would "do away with all the patriotism we have."[56] James Griffin believed that "this is quite an unfortunate time for all these changes, inasmuch as we are in sight of the Enemy, and may be attacked at any moment."[57] One unit, Dreux's Battalion, was actually set to disband on 11 April, but Magruder personally pleaded with the Louisianans, stating, "That it may never be said that a La. Battalion… moved to the rear at the sound of the enemy's cannon."[58] The battalion only disbanded when Johnston ordered the retreat from the Peninsula. The local regiment, 32nd Virginia, held its reorganization while in the trenches. New officers were selected for the Warwick Beauregards (Company H), as well as other companies. The men were rather dissatisfied, and when the army retreated toward Richmond, many soldiers, like Privates David and Edward Hopkins of New Kent County, simply deserted. Overall, the elections were often tainted by "whiskey, promises and bribes of various sorts."[59] "Passed the whiskey round and opened the polls," wrote Private John Tucker of the 5th Alabama, "a great many of the men got gloriously drunk."[60]

Both armies continued to exert pressure on each other's positions, particularly where the Warwick River reached its headwaters. Magruder had constructed a complex system of earthworks to guard against any advance that might break through the Confederate lines. Fort Magruder (also known as the White Redoubt) was a lunette and, along with the Red Redoubt, was built to stop any enemy passing the head of a series of ravines that contained rivulets that formed the headwaters of the Warwick River. Trenches and epaulments ran from the Red Redoubt to the Wynne's Mill earthworks. Brigadier General John Wynn Davidson's command was involved in two minor skirmishes near Wynne's Mill. Davidson, an 1854 West Point graduate and native Virginian who decided to remain loyal to the Union, sent troops to disrupt Confederate picket posts on 19 April 1862. On 22 April, the Confederates retaliated when prewar lawyer Colonel Christopher Haynes Mott sent about two hundred men from his 19th Mississippi Regiment to probe the Federal lines at 12:00 a.m.

Elements of the 7th Maine, commanded by Captain Morse, were gathered and forced the Confederates back through the dense woods across the river. Davidson lauded Morse as well as several of those killed during the engagement. He noted that one of the Maine soldiers was killed by a volley, with at least twenty balls in his body. Another soldier, the mortally wounded George O. McLellan, loaded his gun and fired it at the enemy and then applied his own handkerchief as a tourniquet.[61]

Brigadier General Cuvier Grover organized another assault against a lunette on the south side of the head of the Warwick River. Company M, 1st Massachusetts Regiment, crossed a six-hundred-yard open field and took the earthwork without firing a shot. The Confederates inflicted sixteen casualties on the Federals. Most of the Confederates ran at the Union advance; however, fourteen were captured. Grover's men broke down most of the earthwork's parapet. Realizing that there were numerous other Confederate defenses nearby, though, they fell back to their own lines. When McClellan advised Edwin Stanton of the action, he sent the Union general a telegram stating, "I am rejoiced to learn that your operations are progressing so rapidly and with so much spirit and success, and congratulate you and the officers and soldiers engaged upon the brilliant affair."[62]

When the siege entered its fourth week, Joe Johnston started thinking of retreating. On 29 April, Johnston once again advised Richmond that because of McClellan's overwhelming strength in heavy artillery, he could not hold the Peninsula. His divisional commanders generally agreed with this opinion. D.H. Hill believed that the Confederates could only withstand a two-day bombardment, but Johnston felt otherwise, stating "about two hours."[63] Army of the Potomac Chief of Artillery William F. Barry thought that the fire of the entire Union siege "would have compelled the enemy to surrender or abandon his works in less than twelve hours."[64] While Johnston planned his evacuation, Lee endeavored to prompt the *Virginia* to attack the Federal vessels threatening Yorktown. Flag Officer Josiah Tattnall, the ironclad's new commander, simply would not risk his ironclad, citing that

Union ordnance at Yorktown. *Courtesy of the U.S. Army Military Historical Institute.*

his ship was too unseaworthy to steam past Fort Monroe and then have to face the entire Union fleet. The sixty-seven-year-old Josiah Tattnall was a legendary naval hero. He gained distinction during the War of 1812's Battle of Craney Island on 22 June 1813 and was lauded for his service at Vera Cruz during the Mexican War, receiving a gold sword from his native state of

Georgia. He was a seasoned veteran who reluctantly resigned his commission when Georgia seceded. On 21 March 1862, Tattnall was named to replace Franklin Buchanan as commander of the James River Defenses, with the CSS *Virginia* as his flagship. Although noted for his aggressive tactics, Josiah Tattnall recognized the Confederate ironclad's limitations. The Union had by now added two more ironclads, USS *Galena* and the iron-hulled *Naugatuck*, to join the USS *Monitor*. Tattnall advised both Lee and Mallory that the *Virginia* would be handled "with proper prudence" to halt any Union move toward Norfolk or up the James River.[65]

Meanwhile, McClellan was making his final preparations for his grand bombardment, which he expected to unleash on 6 May. This plan, according to General Barnard, was to have all the batteries ready by the evening of 5 May, and on the next day, several batteries would concentrate on Wynne's Mill, Red Redoubt and Fort Magruder, while the strongest batteries (Nos. 1, 2, 10, 13 and 14) would strike at the Yorktown and Gloucester Point batteries. Once these Confederate batteries had been reduced, the Union gunboats could pass the York River narrows and open fire on Yorktown's rear and at the passage of the Yorktown-Williamsburg Road. Barnard believed that "the forcing of such a line with so little loss…is an exploit

Confederate water battery, Yorktown, Virginia. *Courtesy of the U.S. Army Military Historical Institute.*

less brilliant perhaps, but more worthy of study, than would have been a murderous assault, even if it had proved successful."[66] Actually, the Federals tested the range of Battery No. 1 on 1 May 1862, firing 141 rounds into Yorktown and the wharves along the waterfront. Transports rushed away up the York. Johnston realized that his army could not escape by water and that the time was at hand to leave the Warwick-Yorktown line. Brigadier General William B. Franklin's division, which had been on board transports since its arrival in the York River on 22 April, was disembarked at Wormley Creek on 2 May to give greater force to the eventual infantry assault against the Confederate line. McClellan had given up hope of running these troops past the York River batteries with the *Galena* prior to his bombardment. The U.S. Navy simply refused to move up the river until the Confederate batteries on both sides of the river were disabled. McClellan, nonetheless, expected the Southern forces to try to hold their Peninsula defenses. He was confident of his eventual victory as he advised Lincoln, "I see the way clear to success and hope to make it brilliant, although with but little loss of life."[67]

But the drama was not to end as McClellan expected. Joe Johnston began advising Richmond that retreat was necessary when he wrote Lee on 27 April:

> *The weather is most unpropitious; the roads as bad as possible. The march of our army with its wagons and artillery would be very difficult. The passage of the Federal army up York River would render a rapid movement necessary on our part. Do urge the work on the bridges of the Chickahominy.*[68]

Johnston ordered the withdrawal of his army on 2 May, but poor staff work, bad weather and muddy roads delayed the retreat. The order had not taken many Confederates by surprise, as James Griffin wrote his wife on 28 April, "I don't think this is the place for us to fight…I wouldn't be surprised if our army falls back from here."[69] Others, however, were disheartened by the prospects of abandoning the Peninsula, particularly Magruder. Prince John spent his last hours on the Peninsula ill in bed, dismayed by his 2 May orders to move his troops toward Richmond, as one of his staff, Hugh Thomas Douglas, recounted:

> *I shall never forget the morning that General Magruder, lying on his sick bed worn out by the arduous duties of three weeks, a strain enough to have killed any ordinary man, summoned me to his room and directed me to prepare for the move. The tears coursed down the old man's cheeks and*

Confederate dismounted cannon, Yorktown, Virginia. *Courtesy of the U.S. Army Military Historical Institute.*

> *rising on one arm with dramatic effect, he pointed to his little army, and said "Sic transit Gloria, Peninsula."*[70]

On the evening of 3 May, the Confederates unleashed a tremendous bombardment to cover their retreat toward Williamsburg. By morning, the trenches were empty.

The Federal command was caught off balance by this unexpected Confederate withdrawal. The Union soldiers, however, were jubilant that the siege was now over. Soldiers raced to win everlasting glory by placing their unit's colors first atop the Confederate earthworks. Edward Wilson of Birney's Zouaves achieved this honor when he affixed the Stars and Stripes on the crest of the Lee's Mill battlements.[71] As the soldiers entered the

Confederate positions, they were shocked to discover the subterra torpedoes left behind to retard their advance. Developed by Brigadier General Gabriel J. Rains, these land mines were actually 8- or 10-inch Columbiad shells, buried a few inches under the soil and set with primers so that they exploded when stepped on or moved. It was the first use of this controversial weapon during the Civil War, and these buried shells injured scores of Union soldiers. As Richard Derby wandered through the abandoned works at Yorktown to observe a burst Confederate cannon, a nearby soldier "trod on a torpedo, and the shell exploded, throwing him ten feet into the air, tearing off one leg, burning him black as a negro."[72] At Lee's Mill, Private Albert Berry of the 23rd Pennsylvania was able to save the life of a Sergeant Caldwell when Caldwell stepped on a torpedo, triggering its fuse. Berry acted quickly to empty his canteen on it, thereby putting it out. McClellan was shocked by this barbaric weapon, and since torpedoes were delaying the advance of his troops, he "ordered that they should be discovered and removed by the Confederate prisoners."[73]

Union soldiers posing with an exploded Confederate cannon, Yorktown, Virginia. *Courtesy of the U.S. Army Historical Institute.*

Despite the torpedoes, the Union soldiers were amazed by the abandoned extensive works, military stores, camps and huge siege guns left behind by the Confederates. Johnston had left behind fifty-six heavy cannons (three of these had burst during the night bombardment on 3 May) and ammunition for these guns without damaging any of this ordnance; however, he was able to remove all of the field pieces. The Confederate general was strongly criticized for his retreat, and many compared it to how he had left Manassas just two months before. Nevertheless, Lieutenant Edgar N. Newcomb of the 19th Massachusetts found perhaps the most telling memento left behind by the Confederates written on an abandoned tent: "He that fights and runs away, will live to fight another day. May 3."[74]

The four-week siege had long-lasting implications. McClellan's initial hesitation in front of Magruder's defenses gave the Confederacy time to mobilize its forces for its defense of Richmond. Even though McClellan did not take advantage of breaking the Confederate lines on several occasions early in the siege (notably on 16 April at the Battle of Dam No. 1), it is the presence of the CSS *Virginia* that enabled the siege to last as long as it did. The Federal navy believed that it could not support an attack against the York River batteries, an action that could have broken the siege by flanking the Confederate defenses, because it had to protect McClellan's army from the *Virginia*.

The Union command had no knowledge of the *Virginia*'s numerous weaknesses nor the fact that the Confederate batteries defending the James River were not as strong or well positioned as those on the York. The Federal navy simply did not act resolutely in support of McClellan. Denied the use of the James River, concerned about casualties and desirous of reinforcements, McClellan felt that he had no alternative but to besiege the imposing Confederate works. Although often criticized for his retreat from the Peninsula, Joseph Johnston was right that his defenses could not withstand McClellan's planned bombardment. While he saved his army from possible destruction, Johnston's hurried retreat would have a telling impact on the Confederate control of Hampton Roads.

9

Consequences

A few months after the siege was over, John Bankhead Magruder wrote his report detailing his army's defense of the Peninsula:

> *From April 4 to May 3 this army served almost without relief in the trenches. It rained incessantly; the trenches were filled with water. The weather was exceedingly cold; no fires could be allowed; the artillery and infantry of the enemy played down upon our men almost continuously day and night; the army had neither coffee, sugar, nor hard bread, but subsisted on flour and salt meat, and that in reduced quantities, and yet no murmurs were heard.*[1]

The siege may have been a heroic stand against insurmountable odds, but as the Confederate troops marched along the muddy roads, they left behind them a Union army and navy ready to strike.

McClellan was just about finished with his final preparations for his grand bombardment, which he expected to unleash on 5 May. Once he had destroyed the Confederate water batteries with his heavy Parrott guns and seacoast mortars, he intended to attack Yorktown with Heintzelman's III Corps. The USS *Galena* would steam past the batteries and flank the Confederate defenses. "I see the way clear to success and hope to make it brilliant," McClellan had advised Lincoln, "although with little loss of life."[2] McClellan had just removed Brigadier General William B. Franklin's division from transports to add punch to the infantry attack.

Consequences

Even though McClellan was caught off guard by Johnston's retreat, he immediately organized a pursuit. The Union general spent most of Sunday, 4 May, preparing Franklin's 11,300-man division to be back on its transports so that these troops could be rushed up the York River to Eltham's Landing to cut off the Confederate retreat. He also created a strike force, a corps des chasseurs, under the command of Brigadier General Edwin Vose Sumner, to intercept the Confederate rear guard before it reached beyond Williamsburg. The Union advance guard of cavalry and light artillery clashed with Brigadier General J.E.B. Stuart's cavalry at Lee Hall and Skiffes Creek Bridge and along King's Creek. Brigadier General George Stoneman pressed the Confederates back to where the two main roads coming up the Peninsula converged just outside Williamsburg. As darkness began to shroud the crossroads and Federal infantry arrived on the scene, the Confederates were able to take refuge behind the series of redoubts that Magruder had built months before.

General Johnston was in a rush to get his supply train and artillery beyond the Chickahominy River. The Confederate retreat was "much impeded by the slow movement of the wagon trains over the miry roads, was tardy and tedious in the extreme." Vines Turner later commented that the rain-soaked Peninsula roads were nothing but "mud and slush" and that "the tenacious mire was often knee deep. Shoes were pulled from our feet by it and lost. Pantaloons became so caked and weighted with mud that many, in sheer desperation and utter inability… cut off and threw away all below the knee."[3] Johnston sensed that McClellan might move troops up to the head of the York River to block his retreat from Richmond. He needed to move all his equipment and men quickly through the mud westward to the Confederate capital. Consequently, he placed Major General James Longstreet in command of the Confederate defenses. Longstreet, in turn, ordered Brigadier General Richard Heron Anderson, an 1842 West Point graduate, to hold the Confederate

Brigadier General J.E.B. Stuart, CSA.
Courtesy of the Museum of the Confederacy.

Confederate retreat from Yorktown. *Courtesy of the Virginia Historical Society.*

Brigadier General Richard Heron Anderson, CSA. *Courtesy of U.S. Army Military Historical Institute.*

lines around Fort Magruder. Anderson had two brigades to thwart any Union advance.

At dawn on 5 May 1862, Brigadier General Joseph Hooker had his troops ready to assault. The Union troops made little headway against Fort Magruder. The rain, mud and fierce Confederate resistance stymied the Federal advance. As the sound of the battle grew louder, Joe Johnston returned to Fort Magruder to ascertain the combat situation. Longstreet sensed an opportunity to achieve a stunning victory. Johnston agreed; a counterattack was organized, and it struck the Federal left flank and pressed the Federals back. Hooker tried to rally his men; however, General Heintzelman came forward and ordered a bewildered band to play. "Play! Play! It's all you're good for," he exclaimed. "Play, damn it! Play some marching tune! Play 'Yankee Doodle' or any doodle you can think of, only play something!"[4] Amid the rain, thunder and sound of battle came strains of music, which helped to stabilize the Federals.

Nevertheless, the battle began in favor of the Federals when Brigadier General Philip Kearny's division arrived from Yorktown. Kearny, who had lost his left arm during the Mexican War, was called by Winfield Scott "the bravest man I ever saw, and a perfect soldier."[5] Kearny had served in Emperor Louis Napoleon's Imperial Guard and was awarded the Legion of Honor. Phil Kearny had just been placed in command of his division, and he rushed his troops forward to the sound of battle. As he led his men into the fray, he shouted, "I am a one-armed Jersey son-of-a-gun; follow me!" Kearny personally reconnoitered the front and announced, "Men, I want you to drive those black guards to hell at once!"[6] The troops surged forward and retook the captured Federal batteries. Soon, the Confederates were forced back into Fort Magruder, and the line stabilized to the morning's positions.

Sumner had received information from a contraband earlier in the day that the Confederate left was unprotected. Four redoubts were not manned

Brigadier General Philip Kearny, USA. *Courtesy of the Library of Congress.*

by Johnston's troops. Neither Johnston nor Longstreet knew the complete extent of the Williamsburg Line, which contained a total of fourteen redoubts. The most critical position was Redoubt #14, which guarded the important passage over the milldam on Cub Creek, a tributary of Queen's Creek. Sumner sent Brigadier General Winfield Scott Hancock with his brigade and artillery. As Kearny attacked at Fort Magruder, Hancock positioned his men virtually behind Fort Magruder in front of Redoubt #11 and began to shell the Confederate positions. Hancock called for reinforcements; however, Sumner ordered him to fall back, and he refused to send additional troops. Sumner, who had been in the Union army since 1819, was totally confused about Hancock's tactical opportunity, which prompted the Comte de Paris to state that he witnessed Sumner during the battle and thought that "the grand old man, wizened, white-bearded, has an air of stupidity that perfectly expresses his mental state."[7]

Brigadier General Winfield Scott Hancock, USA. *Courtesy of the Library of Congress.*

Brigadier General Jubal Anderson Early, CSA. *Courtesy of the Museum of the Confederacy.*

Hancock's shelling alerted Longstreet to the threat. Unfortunately, he had already committed all of his troops into action around Fort Magruder. He requested support from Major General D.H. Hill's division. Hill picked Brigadier General Jubal Anderson Early's brigade to counter the danger posed by Hancock's occupation of Redoubt #11. Early commanded the left wing, consisting of the 24th and 38th Virginia, while Hill led the 23rd and 5th North Carolina on the right. The brigade marched into the dense woods toward the sound of Hancock's artillery. The regiments lost their alignment and direction as the men struggled through the thick underbrush and heavy rain. Early and the 24th Virginia were the first to gain the clearing, but it was more than 600 yards in front, rather than on the flank of Hancock's Brigade. Early, instead of waiting for the rest of the brigade, wheeled his men about and marched toward the Federals.

Hancock, whose men were just preparing to comply with Sumner's orders to fall back to the Union lines, told his men, "Charge, gentlemen, charge."[8] The Federals charged "with a terrible yell…and poured in a volley."[9] The Confederates were hit with a telling fire. Jubal Early was shot through the shoulder and had to be removed from the field, faint from loss of blood, all the while urging his men forward. Hill then emerged onto the field with the 5th North Carolina and recognized that he needed to support the Virginians. Even though the 38th Virginia and 23rd North Carolina were still entangled in the woods, Hill ordered the 5th to move forward through the Custis wheat field, which was recalled as "the valley of death."

Major Peter Sinclair wrote, "Our line was as perfect and unbroken as if on parade, at each step our gallant boys would fall." Sinclair added that he had never heard of anything that surpassed it in bravery.[10] However, Hill ordered a halt to the "fatally destructive and disjointed assault." The Confederates had suffered grievous casualties. "The slaughter of the 5th North Carolina was one of the most awful things I ever saw,"[11] Hill recounted. Indeed, the unit had suffered a casualty rate of 68 percent. Hill's crippled strike force fell back in defeat as darkness began to shroud the battlefield. The inconclusive Battle of Williamsburg was over.

McClellan called the Battle of Williamsburg "an accident" caused by too rapid a pursuit. The Confederates suffered 1,603 casualties, with over half of them, 810 men, killed or wounded during the fatal attack against Hancock's brigade. The Federals lost 2,239 men, killed, wounded or missing on that stormy May day. "Hancock was superb," McClellan wired to Washington, D.C. The Army of the Potomac had at last fought a major battle, and McClellan declared that the "victory is complete." McClellan arrived on the battlefield as the last shots were being fired. "The Men cheered like friends," McClellan later told his wife, "and I saw at once that I had saved the day."[12] Joe Johnston had a different interpretation of the battle, as he later wrote, "Had the enemy beaten us on the fifth, as he claims to have done, our army

Battle of Williamsburg, 5 May 1862. *Courtesy of John Moran Quarstein.*

would have lost most of its baggage and artillery."[13] Though the Federals were able to force the Confederates to abandon Williamsburg, Longstreet's rear-guard action gave Johnston time to move his army toward Richmond. Williamsburg was a mismanaged battle by both commands. Johnston did not understand the true extent of the Williamsburg Line. Unfortunately, Magruder's troops led the way toward Richmond and were not available to either defend or advise about the fortifications they themselves had constructed. Colonel R.L. Maury later wrote:

> *The mistake, growing out of ignorance or carelessness, might have been avoided had General Magruder been assigned to the defense of the rear on that day, for he and his troops were perfectly familiar with the whole country—they had been there the previous autumn and winter and had themselves laid out and built those very fortifications.*[14]

Johnston was so focused on getting his army past the Chickahominy that he did not plan an effective defense of the Williamsburg Line. Nevertheless, this battle blocked the Federal pursuit of the Confederates and enabled Johnston to get his army intact to the outskirts of Richmond. McClellan had once again allowed the Confederate army to escape his grasp. The Confederates escaped, in part, McClellan believed, due to the "utter stupidity and worthlessness of the Corps Commanders… Heaven alone can help a General with such commanders under him." McClellan was particularly displeased with Keyes and Sumner. He felt that Sumner "was a greater fool than I had supposed"[15] and believed that the aged general had almost lost the battle for the Union. The Federals had a reasonable opportunity to crush the Confederate army at Williamsburg. Sumner failed to understand the Federal opportunities to uncover both Confederate flanks nor did he

Brigadier General Edwin Vose Sumner, USA.
Courtesy of the Library of Congress.

realize that he had more than twenty-five thousand soldiers near the battlefield just waiting to be called into action. Union officers like Baldy Smith called for McClellan to come to the front lines to bring order to the command's chaos. McClellan did not begin to ride toward the battlefield until late afternoon, and by then, his opportunity to attain a complete victory was lost.

Nevertheless, the Union thrust against the retreating Confederates did not end at Williamsburg. McClellan had spent most of the day supervising the embarkation of Franklin's division onto transports to cut off the Confederate retreat near Eltham's Landing on the Pamunkey River. The Federal fleet was delayed going up the York River on 4 May

Brigadier General William Buell Franklin, USA. *Courtesy of the U.S. Army Military Historical Institute.*

1862, as Flag Officer Thomas Jefferson Page, CSN, manned the Gloucester Point water battery until 1:00 p.m. His shelling slowed the Federal efforts to rush up the river. Brigadier General William B. Franklin's division finally reached Eltham's Landing on 6 May 1862, a day too late. The Union troops disembarked and entrenched under the protection of the Union gunboats. Joe Johnston reacted quickly to contain this threat by sending Major General Gustavus Woodson Smith's wing of the Confederate army from Barhamsville to Eltham's Landing. Smith ordered Brigadier General William Henry Chase Whiting to press the Federals. Accordingly, Whiting sent Brigadier General John Bell Hood with his Texas Brigade to block any Federal advance. Franklin felt he needed to wait for the arrival of three additional divisions before making any concerted efforts to cut off the Confederate retreat toward Richmond. Therefore, he sent a brigade forward on a reconnaissance mission and kept most of his men positioned at Eltham's Landing, under the protection of Union gunboats. Hood's brigade moved aggressively forward, driving the Federals back on the landing. Franklin reported to McClellan about the Eltham's Landing engagement that "I congratulate myself that we have maintained our position."[16] The Battles of Eltham's Landing cost

186 Union and 48 Confederate casualties and enabled Johnston's army to safely reach the outskirts of Richmond. McClellan had missed yet another opportunity to destroy or disrupt Johnston's retreat to Richmond. Even though his army was on the move, the James River still remained closed to use by the Federals.

President Abraham Lincoln, accordingly, became disenchanted with McClellan's slow progress up the Peninsula and decided to go to Fort Monroe to prompt greater action. Lincoln arrived at Old Point Comfort on the evening of 6 May 1862, accompanied by Secretary of War Edwin Stanton and Secretary of Treasury Salmon Chase. Since McClellan's army was already marching toward Richmond, Lincoln met with Major General John Ellis Wool and Flag Officer Louis M. Goldsborough to organize the capture of Norfolk. On 7 May, Lincoln instructed Goldsborough to simultaneously send a naval force into the James River to attack Confederate river forts and shell the batteries at Sewell's Point into submission. Goldsborough hesitated, complaining that he had an insufficient force; nevertheless, he finally conceded to Lincoln's command.

At daybreak on 8 May 1862, Commander John Rodgers entered the James River with the ironclad USS *Galena* and the wooden steamers *Aroostook* and *Port Royal*. Then Goldsborough sent the ironclads USS *Monitor* and USRMS *Naugatuck* along with the wooden gunboats *Seminole*, *Susquehanna*, *San Jacinto* and *Dacotah* to bombard Sewell's Point. When Flag Officer Josiah Tattnall heard the shelling, he immediately steamed down the Elizabeth River to contest the Union advance. As the *Virginia* neared Sewell's Point, Tattnall realized that he faced a difficult decision. He could either send his ironclad to block Rodgers's advance up the James River or he could protect the Confederate batteries defending Norfolk. Since Rodgers was, by now, far enough up the James River where the *Virginia* could not reach (due to her tremendous draft), and due to the peremptory need to protect his base, Tattnall steamed toward the *Monitor* and the other ships. While it appeared that a second contest between the two ironclads might occur, Goldsborough ordered the Federal Squadron to withdraw beyond Fort Monroe. Tattnall continued to steam around Hampton Roads for the next two hours, hoping that he might induce the *Monitor* to attack. Finally, Tattnall, disgusted by the Union's lack of aggression, ordered Catesby Jones to "fire a gun to windward and take the ship back to her buoy." This act of disdain and defiance was considered most appropriate by the *Virginia*'s crew, as John Taylor Wood noted, "It was the most cowardly exhibition I have ever seen… Goldsborough and Jeffers are two cowards."[17]

Consequences

CSS *Virginia* forcing the retreat of the Union squadron at Sewell's Point, Virginia, off Craney Island, Virginia, 8 May 1862. *Courtesy of John Moran Quarstein.*

President Abraham Lincoln watched the entire action from Fort Wool and was disappointed with the U.S. Navy's failure to reduce Sewell's Point. The president was also dismayed that the *Monitor* did not engage the Confederate ironclad, even though Lincoln had previously ordered that the *Monitor* not combat the *Virginia*. Nevertheless, Lincoln's two-pronged naval assault was successful. Rodgers was up the James River and had silenced Fort Boykin and Fort Huger on the south side of the river. Norfolk was now isolated and the James River open, apparently all the way to Richmond.

Lincoln recognized that Norfolk could not be taken by naval assault, so he made personnel reconnaissance of the coastline east of Sewell's Point. He selected Ocean View as the place to organize a landing. General Wool assembled a task force of six thousand men and, using canalboats, sent these men in two waves, beginning on the evening of 9 May. The advance force was commanded by Brigadier General J.K.F. Mansfield. The troops were disembarked, which prompted Major General Benjamin Huger to evacuate Norfolk. The *Virginia* was left isolated and without a homeport. Unfortunately, the Confederates could not adequately lighten their ironclad enough to be taken upriver to Richmond. Tattnall, therefore, decided to run the huge ironclad aground at Craney Island and then scuttled her. As Chief Engineer Ashton Ramsay later lamented, "Still unconquered, we hauled down our dropping colors, their laurels all fresh and green, and with mingled pride and grief gave her to the flames."[18] The Federals rejoiced, and the James River path to Richmond was completely opened. The *Virginia's* crew was then sent to the ninety-foot-high Drewry's Bluff, eight miles below Richmond. There, along with the Southside Artillery and Bedford Artillery, the *Virginia's* crew stopped the *Monitor, Galena, Naugatuck, Aroostook* and *Port Royal* from reaching Richmond. The first phase of the Peninsula Campaign was over.

The *Virginia's* ability to defend Norfolk and the James River approach to Richmond from March until early May 1862 had a major impact on McClellan's Peninsula Campaign. It was delayed and altered by the Confederate ironclad's mere existence. The U.S. Navy simply did not recognize the *Virginia's* limitations. Consequently, Flag Officer Goldsborough suffered from "ram fever," or, as William Keeler described the malaise, "*Merrimac*-on-the-brain."

Destruction of CSS *Virginia*, off Craney Island, Virginia, 11 May 1862. *Courtesy of John Moran Quarstein.*

Consequences

George McClellan had developed a brilliant plan using all the assets that the Federals had available to capture Richmond. His prior experience enabled him to understand how to use naval superiority to operate along an enemy's coast. Without effective naval support, McClellan had no other choice but to rely on his own resources to move past the Confederate defenses on the Peninsula. Unfortunately for McClellan, his initial plan to capture Yorktown was based on faulty maps and intelligence. Despite the Confederate high command's opinion of McClellan's "high attainments and capacity," Magruder was undaunted by either McClellan's reputation or huge army. Magruder displayed the greatest bluff of the Civil War along the Warwick River as he fooled McClellan. In many ways, McClellan was ready to be deceived and welcomed the opportunity to besiege the Warwick-Yorktown Line to exhibit his engineering prowess. Even though McClellan could have probably broken through Magruder's line, particularly at Dam No. 1, his mindset prompted him to avoid the high casualties caused by aggressive tactics and achieve victory via siege.

The siege would witness the deployment of a variety of innovations that had never been previously utilized in warfare. McClellan's siege guns, particularly the heavy rifled Parrotts, were the most powerful weapons ever assembled against an enemy. Yorktown would have been utterly destroyed had not the Confederate army slipped away forty-eight hours before the bombardment was slated to begin. The Army of the Potomac commander had brought with him everything that could enhance his success. The use of the Agar Gun was the first time such a rapid-fire gun accompanied an army. McClellan was innovative in his organization of transports and a complex supply system to support his huge army in the field. He was so well prepared to move against the Confederate capital that he had brought locomotives and cars with his army to operate on the Richmond & York River Railroad.

Likewise, the Confederates shared several new technologies with the Federals, including balloons and ironclads. Balloons were a unique feature of the siege and helped both sides gain knowledge about enemy positions. The ironclads were perhaps the most influential. The CSS *Virginia* reintroduced the ram to naval warfare. The *Cumberland* was the first warship sunk by ramming in modern warfare; the ram would remain a key design feature of warships for the next 40 years. The *Virginia*'s antagonist on 9 March, the USS *Monitor*, introduced the turret to warship design, a feature still found on warships 150 years afterward. The other Union ironclads were not as influential. The six-gun USS *Galena* had insufficient iron plating and was

Ayres's Battery crossing Dam No. 1, 4 May 1862. *Courtesy of the Vermont Historical Society.*

badly damaged during the 15 May 1862 Battle of Drewry's Bluff. The USRMS *Naugatuck* had an iron hull; however, her 100-pounder Parrott rifle was operated en barbette, which provided no protection whatsoever for her gun crew. The U.S. Navy also introduced the submarine USS *Alligator*. Commanded by Lieutenant Thomas O. Selfridge, who had served aboard the USS *Cumberland* when she was sunk on 8 March and who was a temporary commander of the *Monitor*, the *Alligator* was innovative but impractical. Nevertheless, the battle between the *Virginia* and the *Monitor* changed naval warfare forever. The mere existence of the Confederate ironclad affected McClellan's plans and caused Flag Officer Goldsborough to not support any naval action against Yorktown or Gloucester Point. The failure to employ combined operations against the Warwick-Yorktown Line delayed and disrupted McClellan's hope for a rapid march against Richmond. The Confederates also introduced land mines to warfare. Brigadier General Gabriel Rains's "subterra torpedoes" caused indignation on both sides and were not deployed again until the siege of Petersburg.

All these technologies were features of the first siege of the Civil War. The lunettes, redoubts, redans and rifle pits introduced this model of warfare exactly where the Franco-American army had cornered and captured Lord Cornwallis, effectively ending the Revolutionary War. Thoughts about the 19 October 1781 victory at Yorktown were considered by Northern and Southern soldiers alike. Magruder made reference to Yorktown as a key to victory "in this second war of independence."[19] George McClellan referenced the Revolutionary siege often at the beginning of his campaign. The Union general wrote to President Lincoln and Secretary of War Edwin Stanton that he intended to encircle and capture Magruder's army just as Washington had done to Lord Cornwallis. Philip Kearny recalled that an old slave, at least ninety years old, remembered hearing the sound of cannon fire at Yorktown in 1781. Confederate soldiers actually rebuilt some of Cornwallis's fortifications, and Union officers referred to old maps of the first siege of Yorktown to gather clues to the placement of their artillery. "The graphic pen of the historian has rendered it unnecessary for me to say much of a place so famous in American history where the last blows of independence was struck," wrote J. Lee of the 2nd Louisiana. "It is a hallowed spot where the hellish persecutor of tyranny—Cornwallis—surrendered his sword."[20] Another Confederate, known only by his initials, J.R.G., recounted:

> We were encamped on the battlefield near Yorktown. Within a few hundred yards, and in full view of our camp, stands the monument where Lord Cornwallis surrendered his sword, still nearer is the [Moore] house in which the terms of his capitulation were signed. It is a staunch looking building—might stand the shock of another battle or revolution, and witness the capitulation of another invading general.[21]

Vines Edmunds Turner reflected on his "service at Yorktown":

> About the quaint old town were many points of interest that awakened patriotic contemplation. The marble slab half a mile from town, marking the spot where eighty years before Cornwallis had surrendered to Washington, was a favorite place of visitation. Standing there on consecrated ground many a fond prayer was breathed that this self-same spirit which witnessed the achievement of American Independence might also see the accomplishment of Southern Independence.[22]

Cornwallis Cave, Yorktown, Virginia, May 1862. *Courtesy of the U.S. Army Military Historical Institute.*

The Confederates looked upon Yorktown as where their independence could be won, while the Federals believed it to be the place where the nation could be preserved.

The second siege of Yorktown did not have the same impact as General George Washington's victory in 1781. The month-long siege gave the Confederates time to muster more troops for the defense of Richmond and allowed them to hold Norfolk, enabling the Confederates to launch a new ironclad, the CSS *Richmond*, at Gosport Navy Yard. Although this ironclad was far from complete when she was towed to Richmond, the *Richmond* would eventually help defend the Confederate capital. The Confederates' retreat, however, meant that all of Hampton Roads would be controlled by the

Federals. The region's vast agricultural, harbor and shipbuilding resources were now able to support the Union efforts to capture Richmond and control the Confederate coastline. Even though the Federals now controlled most of Tidewater Virginia, Richmond was saved. The war would last another bloody three years.

The siege of the Warwick-Yorktown Line had a major impact on the careers of the three commanding generals. Even though McClellan was able to display his brilliant understanding of siege warfare, it became apparent during the siege and its immediate aftermath that McClellan was not a combat leader. He refused to launch concerted assaults against several Confederate weak points along the Warwick River and arrived late on the Williamsburg Battlefield. McClellan thought it was more important to coordinate the landing of Franklin's division onto transports than to supervise the battle that he could hear rumbling eight miles away. This pattern would become evident as the campaign evolved into the Seven Days Battles. "Curiously enough," Lieutenant Colonel Francis Palfrey of the 20th Massachusetts later wrote, "there was almost always something for McClellan to do than fight his own battles."[23] McClellan was a great strategist and engineer but faltered when the killing began. His inability to capture Richmond and failure to press Lee's army after the 17 September 1862 Battle of Sharpsburg resulted in his removal as commander of the Army of the Potomac. He never again held a command during the war.

Joe Johnston's reputation would not be enhanced by the siege. Even though he complied with Jefferson Davis's wishes to move his army to the Lower Peninsula as quickly as he could, Johnston's retreat was disorganized. Yet despite all the equipment and armament left behind, he was able to successfully move his army to the outskirts of Richmond. He wanted to have a great battle with McClellan, but when the great opportunity came at Seven Pines on 31 May 1862, Johnston was grievously wounded and faded away from the campaigns in Virginia to serve in the West.

Magruder's role in the siege merely reinforced the fame he had earned at Big Bethel. The "Master of Ruses and Strategy" bluffed McClellan into preparing a siege, which gave the Confederacy time to organize its resources to stop McClellan from capturing Richmond. Magruder pulled this bluff again later in the campaign as he held the attention of four of McClellan's corps below the Chickahominy. The first of the Seven Days Battles, the Battle of Oak Grove, was so successful that the Federals were unaware of Robert E. Lee's attack intended for Beaver Dam Creek. Unfortunately, Magruder was unable to effectively handle his command during the battles of Savage

Station and Malvern Hill. Rumors were heard that he was drunk at Malvern Hill. While he was vindicated of this charge, Magruder was transferred to the Trans-Mississippi Department. There, Magruder regained some glory when he liberated Galveston, Texas, on 1 January 1863, and he continued to serve in the West until the war's conclusion.

While Magruder's defense of the Warwick-Yorktown Line was the highlight of his Civil War career, McClellan did not gain the same success on the Lower Peninsula. The CSS *Virginia* proved to be the cause of his difficulties there. The Union's preoccupation with the Confederate ironclad ended any hope of a combined attack against Yorktown and Gloucester Point. Unfortunately, McClellan failed to seize on John Barnard's recommendation that Norfolk be attacked and captured before moving against Richmond. Considering McClellan's fondness for indirect movements and combined operations, it is surprising that he did not follow the Army of the Potomac's chief engineer's advice. Several conditions favored this action. Brigadier General Ambrose E. Burnside's Roanoke Island Expedition had been a major success. Union naval forces occupied Elizabeth City, North Carolina, on 8 February, and troops under his overall command had reached beyond the entrance to the Great Dismal Swamp canal near South Mills, North Carolina, by mid-April. Although Brigadier General Jesse Reno's brigade was repulsed in action at South Mills on 19 April 1862, a concerted Union effort could have threatened Norfolk from its undefended southern approach. As subsequent events proved, McClellan could easily have organized an army-navy assault against Norfolk. R.E. Lee considered this as one of McClellan's opportunities as the Union army began to assemble in Hampton Roads. Norfolk's capture in early April 1862 would have doomed the *Virginia* and uncovered Magruder's Warwick-Yorktown Line, thereby opening the James River for a rapid movement against Richmond. The Confederate capital may have fallen had McClellan followed this course of action. Instead, McClellan focused on Yorktown and conducted the Civil War's first formal siege. The Union general was able to display his great engineering skills; however, the month's delay only favored the Confederacy.

George McClellan's inability to win President Abraham Lincoln's total support for the Peninsula Campaign prompted Lincoln to withhold troops from the Army of the Potomac's movement up the Peninsula. Major General Nathaniel Banks's division was held in the Shenandoah Valley to defend Washington from this avenue of approach, and the rest of Irvin McDowell's I Corps was retained to guard the overland approach. Just as McClellan found his way past the Lower Peninsula, Major General Thomas

Customhouse and ruins of the Ambler House, Yorktown, Virginia, May 1862. *Courtesy of the U.S. Army Military Historical Institute.*

J. Jackson initiated his Valley Campaign in earnest, prompting Lincoln to withhold even more men from the Army of the Potomac's final thrust against Richmond. Since McClellan constantly believed that he was outnumbered by the Confederates, the lack of reinforcements prompted the Union general to be cautious, defensive and prone to rely on engineering as the key tool by which Richmond could be captured. He believed that the reports of the large concentration of Confederate troops during the entire campaign justified his delays, and each success he attained was of even greater importance. The Warwick-Yorktown siege was a miscalculation that slowed his desired rapid march on Richmond to a crawl, causing his campaign to fail.

About 169,000 men served along the Warwick-Yorktown Line during this thirty-day siege, and they left behind them desecration, devastation and destruction. The Peninsula would not fully recover from the destruction wrought by the passing armies. Magruder had practiced a scorched earth policy, and the Union soldiers looted and destroyed many of the remaining houses and farms. Union soldiers may have called the Peninsula "nothing more than a wild wilderness."[24] However, the Federal troops themselves helped to turn the region into a wasteland. As W.H.T. Squires observed after the war:

> *Where broad acres of tobacco trembled, deep-green and golden, in years of peace and plenty, and stately rows of Indian corn lifted their fronds in martial array, thickets of weeds and underbrush had now unchallenged possession where once a modest cottage sheltered the farmer and his growing family, a ruined chimney, like a sundried skeleton, haunted the farm…Poverty, wretchedness, hunger, death, and despair clutched the heart of the land.[25]*

Even as the beat of the drums faded along the Warwick in May 1862, the second siege of Yorktown left behind an indelible mark on the landscape and the events that followed in Virginia that pivotal year.

Order of Battle

5 APRIL 1862, BATTLE OF LEE'S MILL

SMITH'S DIVISION: BRIGADIER GENERAL WILLIAM F. SMITH

First Brigade: Brigadier General Winfield Scott Hancock
5th Wisconsin
6th Maine
43rd New York
49th Pennsylvania

Second Brigade: Brigadier General W.T.H. Brooks
2nd Vermont
3rd Vermont
4th Vermont
5th Vermont
6th Vermont

Third Brigade: Brigadier General John W. Davidson
7th Maine
33rd New York
49th New York
77th New York

Artillery: Captain Romeyn B. Ayres
1st New York Battery
3rd New York Battery
Battery E, 1st New York
Battery F, 5th United States

MCLAWS'S DIVISION: BRIGADIER GENERAL LAFAYETTE MCLAWS

August's Brigade: Colonel T.P. August
5th Louisiana
10th Louisiana
10th Georgia
15th Virginia

Artillery: Captain Joseph Cosnahan
Peninsula Artillery, 1st Virginia Artillery Regiment

16 APRIL 1862, BATTLE OF DAM NO. 1

SMITH'S DIVISION: BRIGADIER GENERAL WILLIAM F. SMITH

First Brigade: Brigadier General Winfield Scott Hancock
5th Wisconsin
6th Maine
43rd New York
49th Pennsylvania

Second Brigade: Brigadier General W.T.H. Brooks
2nd Vermont
3rd Vermont
4th Vermont
5th Vermont
6th Vermont

Third Brigade: Brigadier General John W. Davidson
7th Maine
33rd New York
49th New York
77th New York

Artillery: Captain Romeyn B. Ayres
1st New York Battery
3rd New York Battery
Battery E, 1st New York
Battery F, 5th United States

McLaws's Division: Brigadier General Lafayette McLaws

Cobb's Brigade: Brigadier General Howell Cobb
16th Georgia
11th Georgia
Cobb's Legion
2nd Louisiana
17th Mississippi
15th North Carolina

Anderson's Brigade: Brigadier General George T. Anderson
7th Georgia
8th Georgia

August's Brigade: Colonel T.P. August
10th Louisiana
15th Virginia

Artillery: Colonel Henry Cabell, 1st Virginia Artillery
Troup Artillery, Cobb's Georgia Legion
1st Company, Richmond Howitzers
Magruder Light Artillery
1st Company, Washington Artillery of New Orleans
2nd Company, Washington Artillery of New Orleans

Artillery in the Peninsula Campaign

UNION ARTILLERY AT YORKTOWN

Field Artillery

MODEL	BORE DIAMETER (inches)	TUBE WT. (pounds)	PROJECTILE WT. (pounds)	RANGE (yards)
12-pounder Napoleon Smoothbore	4.62	1,227	12.30	1,619
10-pounder Parrott Rifle	3.00	890	9.50	1,850
20-pounder Parrott Rifle	3.67	1,750	20.00	1,900

Siege and Garrison Artillery

4.5-inch Rifle	4.50	3,450	33.00	2,078
30-pounder Parrott Rifle	4.20	4,200	29.00	2,200
8-inch Howitzer	8.00	2,614	50.50	1,241
8-inch Mortar	8.00	930	44.50	1,200
10-inch Mortar	10.00	1,852	87.50	2,100

Seacoast Artillery

MODEL	BORE DIAMETER (inches)	TUBE WT. (pounds)	PROJECTILE WT. (pounds)	RANGE (yards)
100-pounder Parrott Rifle	6.40	9,700	100.00	2,247
200-pounder Parrott Rifle	8.00	16,300	175.00	2.000
10-inch Mortar	10.00	5,775	87.50	4,250
13-inch Mortar	13.00	17,120	220.00	4,325

UNION BATTERIES AT YORKTOWN

Battery No. 1

In front of the Farinholt's house, on the right bank of Wormley's Creek, and at its junction with the York River, to command the waterfront of Yorktown and Gloucester and the extreme left of the enemy's land-side works.

Armament: Two 200-pounder Parrott rifled guns; five 100-pounder Parrott rifled guns.

Garrison: One battery, 1st Connecticut Artillery (Captain Burke), Major Kellogg commanding.

Battery No. 2

In front of the enemy's line bearing on Yorktown and Hampton stage road in first parallel.

Armament: Three 4.5-inch rifled siege guns; six 30-pounder Parrott rifled guns; six 20-pounder Parrott rifled guns.

Garrison: Two batteries 1st Connecticut Artillery; one battery 1st Battalion New York Artillery; Major Hemingway, 1st Connecticut Artillery, commanding.

Battery No. 3

In first parallel two hundred yards to the left of Battery No. 2.

Armament: Seven 20-pounder Parrott rifled guns.

Garrison: Two batteries 1st Battalion New York Artillery, Captain Voegelee.

Battery No. 4

In a ravine under plateau of Moore's house.

Armament: Ten 13-inch seacoast mortars.

Garrison: Two batteries 1st Connecticut Artillery (Captains Dow and Harmon), Major Alex Doull, 2nd New York Artillery, commanding.

Battery No. 5

Beyond Warwick Court House stage road, in front of Red Redoubt.

Armament: Eight 20-pounder Parrott rifled guns.

Garrison: Battery E, 2nd U.S. Artillery, Captain Carlisle, and one-half Battery C, 1st Battalion New York Artillery.

Battery No. 6

Junction of Warwick and Hampton Roads.

Armament: Sixteen 10-inch seacoast mortars.

Garrison: One company (Captain Burbank's) 1st Connecticut Artillery.

Battery No. 7

In front of Wynne's Mill.

Armament: Six field 12-pounder cannons.

Battery No. 8

In front of works south of Wynne's Mill.

Armament: Two batteries (twelve guns) of field 12-pounder cannons.

Battery No. 9

To left of old milldam.

Armament: Ten 10-inch siege mortars.

Garrison: Two batteries (Captains Cook and Rockwood) 1st Connecticut Artillery, Major Trumbull commanding.

Battery No. 10

In the middle of first parallel, between right branch and York River.

Armament: Three 100-pounder Parrott rifled guns; one 30-pounder Parrott rifled gun; seven 4.5-inch rifled siege guns.

Garrison: Two companies 5th New York Volunteers, Captain Winslow.

Battery No. 11

At head of ravine E.

Armament: Four 10-inch seacoast mortars.

Garrison: One company 5th New York Volunteers.

Battery No. 12

On Peninsula plateau behind secession huts.

Armament: Five 10-inch seacoast mortars.

Garrison: One company 5th New York Volunteers.

Battery No. 13

To the right of and in front of Moore's house.

Armament: Six 30-pounder Parrott rifled guns.

Garrison: Two companies 5th New York Volunteers, Captain Cambreleng commanding.

Battery No. 14

Extremity (right) of first parallel.

Armament: Three 100-pounder Parrott rifled guns.

Garrison: One battery (Captain Perkins) 1st Connecticut Artillery.

CONFEDERATE RIVER DEFENSES

Fort Boykin: Ten 42-pounder cannons and 32-pounder cannons.

Fort Huger: Thirteen guns mounted: one 10-inch Columbiad rifled cannon, four IX-inch Dahlgren rifled cannons, two 8-inch Columbiad rifled cannons and six hot-shot 32-pounder cannons.

Fort Crafford: Five 42-pounder cannons.

Jamestown Island Battery: Thirteen guns: four IX-inch Dahlgren cannons, four 8-inch Columbiad cannons and five hot-shot 32-pounder cannons.

Yorktown Water Batteries: Twelve 8-inch Columbiads, nine 32-pounder cannons, three IX-inch Dahlgren cannons, one X-inch Dahlgren cannon, one 42-pounder cannon and one 64-pounder cannon.

Gloucester Point: Eight 32-pounder cannons.

Notes

CHAPTER 1

1. U.S. War Department, *War of the Rebellion: A Compilation of the Official Records of the Union and Confederate Armies* (Washington: Government Printing Office, 1880–1901 (hereafter cited as *OR*), 1, 2:23.
2. *Daily Richmond Enquirer*, 22 April 1861.
3. *OR*, 1, 2:612.
4. Ibid., 37.
5. Ibid., 38.
6. Ibid., 93.
7. *New York Times*, 14 June 1861.
8. Faust, *Historical Times Illustrated Encyclopedia*, 468.
9. Lee, "Magruder's Peninsula Campaign in 1862," 64.
10. U.S. Congress, Senate 1 (1848), 263.
11. Cooke, *Stonewall Jackson*, 215.
12. Haskin, *History of the First Regiment of Artillery*, 321.
13. Long, "Memoir of General John Bankhead Magruder," 105 6.
14. J.B. Magruder to R.E. Lee, 18 June 1861.

CHAPTER 2

1. Jensen, *32nd Virginia Infantry*, 3011.
2. *OR*, 1, 2:708–9.
3. *OR*, 1, 4:646.
4. Jensen, *32nd Virginia Infantry*, 41.
5. Styple, *Writing & Fighting from the Army of Northern Virginia*, 12.
6. *OR*, 1, 2:295–96.

7. Ibid.

8. Bradley, "The *Fanny*: First Aircraft Carrier," vol. 2.

9. *New York Tribune*, 3 August 1861.

10. *OR*, 1, 4:467–68.

11. *Richmond Examiner*, 12 August 1861.

12. Hudgins and Kleese, *Recollections of an Old Dominion Dragoon*, 32–33.

13. Jensen, *32nd Virginia Infantry*, 44.

CHAPTER 3

1. *New York Times*, 9 August 1861.

2. Blight, *When This Cruel War Is Over*, 106.

3. *OR*, 1, 4:573.

4. Faust, *Historical Times Illustrated Encyclopedia*, 4.

5. *OR*, 1, 4:573.

6. *OR*, 1, 4:612–13.

7. Corson, *My Dear Jennie*, 34.

8. *OR*, 1, 2:970.

9. Jensen, *32nd Virginia Infantry*, 49.

10. *OR*, 1, 2:970–71.

11. Ibid.

12. *OR*, 1, 51:185.

13. *OR*, 1, 4:680.

14. *OR*, 2, 6:717.

15. Davis, "Mulberry Island and the Civil War," 13.

16. *OR*, 2, 4:644–45.

17. Ibid., 680–81.

18. Ibid., 702.

19. Ibid.

20. Corson, *My Dear Jennie*, 34–35.

21. Ibid., 35; Jensen, *32nd Virginia Infantry*, 46.

22. *OR*, 51, 2:251.

23. Oeffinger, *A Soldier's Journal*, 95.

24. *OR*, 11, 1:403–411.

25. White, *Diary of the War*, 111.

26. *Richmond Dispatch*, 8 June 1861.

27. Oeffinger, *A Soldier's Journal*, 111–12.

28. Benjamin Smith to R.H. Carnae, 25 August 1861.

29. See Jones, *Lee's Tigers*.

30. Leon Jastreminski to "Charlie," 2 September 1861.

31. Oeffinger, *A Soldier's Journal*, 97.

32. Ibid., 98–99.

33. J.B. Magruder to R.E. Lee, 8 August 1861.

34. *OR*, 1, 51, 2:251.

35. Richard Leach to his father, 5 February 1862.
36. Jones, *Lee's Tigers*, 33–34.
37. Bridges, *Lee's Maverick General*, 29.
38. McCash, *Thomas R.R. Cobb*, 267.
39. Casdorph, *Prince John Magruder*, 269.
40. Brent, *Memoirs of the War Between the States*, 231.

CHAPTER 4

1. Sears, *Civil War Papers of George B. McClellan*, 70.
2. Sears, *George B. McClellan*, 95.

CHAPTER 5

1. U.S. Department of the Navy, *Official Records of the Union and Confederate Navies in the War of the Rebellion* (hereafter cited as *ORN*), 2, 2:67.
2. Eggleston, "Captain Eggleston's Narrative," 167.
3. *ORN*, 1, 6:776–77.
4. Phillips, "Career of the Iron-Clad *Virginia*," 201.
5. Wood, "First Fight of the Iron-Clads," vol. 1, 719.
6. Tindall, "True Story of the *Virginia*," 36.
7. Littlepage, "Statement of Midshipman Littlepage," 33.
8. Lewis, *Admiral Franklin Buchanan*, 184.
9. Reaney, "How the Gun-Boat *Zouave* Aided the *Congress*," 714.
10. Quote from lithograph, *The Sinking of the* Cumberland *by the Ironclad* Merrimac, Currier & Ives.
11. Jones, "Services of the *Virginia*," 268.
12. Eggleston, "Captain Eggleston's Narrative," 173.
13. Ramsay, "Most Famous of Sea Duels," 11–12.
14. *ORN*, 1, 6:518.
15. Lewis, "Life on the *Monitor*," 258.
16. Ellis, *The* Monitor *of the Civil War*, 22.
17. Greene, "In the *Monitor* Turret," 1, 720.
18. *OR*, 2, 6:333.
19. *ORN*, 1, 7:99–100.
20. *OR*, 2, 6:334.

CHAPTER 6

1. Sears, *Civil War Papers of George B. McClellan*, 207.
2. Ibid., 215.
3. *ORN*, 1, 7:100.
4. Ibid., 781.

5. Sears, *Civil War Papers of George B. McClellan*, 215.
6. Ibid., 218.
7. *OR*, 2, 3:53.
8. Sears, *Civil War Papers of George B. McClellan*, 217.
9. *OR*, 1, 51:499.
10. Coner, "Letters of Lieutenant Robert M. Miller," 64.
11. *OR*, 1, 51:500.
12. *OR*, 1, 11:389.
13. *OR*, 1, 9:383.
14. *OR*, 1, 9:68.
15. *OR*, 1, 11:405.
16. Ibid., 389.
17. Ibid.
18. Styple, *Writing & Fighting from the Army of Northern Virginia*, 24.
19. *OR*, 1, 11:389.
20. Ibid.
21. Ibid., 406.
22. Patterson, *Yankee Rebel*, 17.
23. McClellan, *McClellan's Own Story*, 254.
24. *OR*, 1, 11:413.
25. Sears, *Civil War Papers of George B. McClellan*, 215.
26. McClellan, *McClellan's Own Story*, 256.
27. *OR*, 1, 11, 1:8.
28. Sears, *Civil War Papers of George B. McClellan*, 217.
29. Ibid.
30. *OR*, 1, 9:358.
31. Rosenblatt and Rosenblatt, *Hard Marching Every Day*, 17.
32. *OR*, 1, 9:358.
33. Blight, *When This Cruel War Is Over*, 109.
34. Norton, *Army Letters*, 57.
35. *OR*, 1, 9:404.
36. Ibid.
37. Barnard, *Peninsular Campaign*, 18.
38. *OR*, 1, 9:404.
39. Barnard, *Peninsular Campaign*, 19.
40. Wainwright, *Diary of Battle*, 58.
41. *OR*, 1, 9:404.
42. Patterson, *Yankee Rebel*, 17.
43. Coner, "Letters of Lieutenant Robert M. Miller," 67.
44. Minnish, "Reminiscences Relating to the Siege of Yorktown," 4.
45. Woodward, *Mary Chesnut's Civil War*, 401.
46. Weymouth, *Memorial Sketch of Lieut. Edgar N. Newcomb*, 54.
47. Lyons, *Soldier's Log*, 26.
48. Sears, *Civil War Papers of George B. McClellan*, 234.
49. Ibid., 245.

Chapter 7

1. Early, *Narrative of the War Between the States*, 59.
2. *OR*, 1, 11:303.
3. Thomas B. Leaver Diary, 2 May 1882.
4. Gilbert Thompson Diary.
5. *OR*, 1, 11:307–8.
6. James Montgomery Holloway Papers, 1861–65.
7. Early, *Narrative of the War Between the States*, 59.
8. Sorrel, *Reflections of a Confederate Staff Officer*, 63.
9. Andrews, *Footprints of a Regiment*, 32–33.
10. Sneden, *Eye of the Storm*, 43.
11. Rosenblatt and Rosenblatt, *Hard Marching Every Day*, 56.
12. Andrews, *Footprints of a Regiment*, 33.
13. Berkley, *Four Years in the Confederate Artillery*, 64.
14. Andrews, *Footprints of a Regiment*, 34.
15. Coner, "Letters of Lieutenant Robert M. Miller," 64.
16. Patterson, *Yankee Rebel*, 17.
17. Blight, *When This Cruel War Is Over*, 118.
18. Sears, *Civil War Papers of George B. McClellan*, 217.
19. Berkley, *Four Years in the Confederate Artillery*, 14.
20. Rhodes, *All for the Union*, 55.
21. Luther Furst Diary, 16 April 1862.
22. *OR*, 1, 11:421.
23. *OR*, 1, 11:406.
24. Webb, *The Peninsula*, 64.
25. Balzar, *Buck's Book*, 29.
26. *OR*, 1, 11:408.
27. Robertson, *Weep Not for Me, Dear Mother*, 72.
28. Balzar, *Buck's Book*, 30.
29. Ibid., 31.
30. Waite, *Vermont in the Great Rebellion*, 125.
31. Robertson, *Weep Not for Me, Dear Mother*, 72–73.
32. *OR*, 1, 11:412.
33. Benedict, *Vermont in the Civil War*, vol. 1, 258.
34. Waite, *Vermont in the Great Rebellion*, 126.
35. Eisenberg, "The 3rd Vermont Has Won a Name," 225.
36. Jones, *Lee's Tigers*, 59.
37. Eisenberg, "The 3rd Vermont Has Won a Name," 227.
38. Rosenblatt and Rosenblatt, *Hard Marching Every Day*, 19.
39. Benedict, *Vermont in the Civil War*, vol. 2, 267.
40. Webb, *The Peninsula*, 66.

CHAPTER 8

1. Minnish, "Reminiscences Relating to the Siege of Yorktown," 4.
2. *OR*, 1, 11:366.
3. Ibid., 473.
4. Johnston, *Narrative of Military Operations During the Civil War*, 116.
5. Coner, "Letters of Lieutenant Robert M. Miller," 79.
6. Andrews, *Footprints of a Regiment*, 33.
7. R. Channing Price Papers.
8. Early, *Narrative of the War Between the States*, 62.
9. Patterson, *Yankee Rebel*, 17.
10. Vines Edmunds Turner Papers.
11. Early, *Narrative of the War Between the States*, 63.
12. McArthur and Burton, *A Gentleman and an Officer*, 199.
13. Norton, *Army Letters*, 68.
14. Blight, *When This Cruel War Is Over*, 111.
15. Patterson, *Yankee Rebel*, 18.
16. McArthur and Burton, *A Gentleman and an Officer*, 199.
17. Andrews, *Footprints of a Regiment*, 33.
18. Vines Edmunds Turner Papers.
19. Donald, *Gone for a Soldier*, 55.
20. Robert E. Lewis Papers.
21. *History of the Twenty-Third Pennsylvania Volunteer Infantry*, 32.
22. Donald, *Gone for a Soldier*, 56.
23. Blight, *When This Cruel War Is Over*, 114.
24. Ritchie, *Four Years in the First New York Light Artillery*, 42.
25. Carroll, *Custer in the Civil War*, 145.
26. Stiles, *Four Years Under Marse Robert*, 145.
27. Vines Edmunds Turner Papers.
28. Early, *Narrative of the War Between the States*, 60–61.
29. Minnish, "Reminiscences Relating to the Siege of Yorktown," 15–16.
30. Noyles, "Letters Written by Sgt. George B. Noyles," 2.
31. Adams, "Letters of James Rush Holmes," 116.
32. Styple, *Letters from the Peninsula*, 51–52.
33. Oeffinger, *A Soldier's Journal*, 139–40.
34. Coner, "Letters of Lieutenant Robert M. Miller," 121.
35. Sears, *Civil War Papers of George B. McClellan*, 235.
36. Custer, "War Memories," 686.
37. Ibid., 685.
38. Ibid.
39. Ibid., 685–86.
40. Ibid.
41. Ibid.
42. Bryan, "Balloon Used for Scout Duty," 33.
43. Ritchie, *Four Years in the First New York Light Artillery*, 43.

44. Bryan, "Balloon Used for Scout Duty," 34–42.

45. Bruce, *Lincoln and the Tools of War*, 199.

46. Lyons, *A Soldier's Log*, 30.

47. Ritchie, *Four Years in the First New York Light Artillery*, 41.

48. Blight, *When This Cruel War Is Over*, 110.

49. Wainwright, *Diary of Battle*, 50.

50. *OR*, 11, 3:449.

51. Oeffinger, *A Soldier's Journal*, 138–39.

52. *OR*, 1, 11:446.

53. *ORN*, 1, 7:765.

54. *OR*, 1, 11:462.

55. Reid, *History of the Fourth Regiment of S.C. Volunteers*, 74.

56. McArthur and Burton, *A Gentleman and an Officer*, 200–201.

57. Jones, *Lee's Tigers*, 60.

58. Ibid.

59. Wilson, "Diary of John S. Tucker," 9.

60. *OR*, 1, 11, 1:382.

61. *OR*, 1, 11, 2:385.

62. Bridges, *Lee's Maverick General*, 7.

63. *ORN*, 1, 7:224.

64. Ibid., 224.

65. *OR*, 1, 11, 2:385.

66. Sears, *Civil War Papers of George B. McClellan*, 247.

67. OR, 1, 11, 1:397.

68. McArthur and Burton, *A Gentleman and an Officer*, 203.

69. H.T. Douglas to S.T.C. Bryan, 29 February 1909.

70. *History of the Twenty-Third Pennsylvania Volunteer Infantry*, 39.

71. Hannaford, *Young Captain Richard C. Derby*, 138.

72. *History of the Twenty-Third Pennsylvania Volunteer Infantry*, 138.

73. Perry, *Infernal Machines*, 27.

74. Weymouth, *Memorial Sketch of Lieut. Edgar N. Newcomb*, 58.

CHAPTER 9

1. *OR*, 1, 11:302.

2. Sears, *Civil War Papers of George B. McClellan*, 247.

3. Vines Edmunds Turner Papers.

4. Samuel Peter Heintzelman Diary, 6 May 1862.

5. Catton, *Army of the Potomac*, 32.

6. Charles B. Haydon Diary, 7 May 1862.

7. Comte de Paris Journal, 12 May 1862.

8. De Joinville, *Army of the Potomac*, 54.

9. Selden Coner to his mother, 8 May 1862.

10. P.J. Sinclair to "Alexander," 12 May 1862.
11. D.H. Hill to Longstreet, 31 August 1885.
12. Sears, *Civil War Papers of George B. McClellan*, 257.
13. Johnston, *Narrative of Military Operations During the Civil War*, 124.
14. Maury, "Battle of Williamsburg," 285.
15. Sears, *Civil War Papers of George B. McClellan*, 257.
16. *OR*, 1, 11, 1:614.
17. Wood, "First Fight of the Ironclads," vol. 1, 710.
18. Ramsay, "Most Famous of Sea Duels," 12.
19. OR, 1, 11, 3:24.
20. Styple, *Writing & Fighting from the Army of Northern Virginia*, 12.
21. Ibid., 21.
22. Vines Edmunds Turner Papers.
23. Palfrey, *Peninsular Campaign of General McClellan*, 96.
24. Williams, "Letters from a Soldier in the Union Army," 15.
25. W.H.T. Squires, *Unleashed at Long Last*, 39.

Bibliography

MANUSCRIPTS AND ARCHIVES

Cary, John B. Letter Book, 16 May–3 August 1861. Eleanor S. Brockenbrough Library, The Museum of the Confederacy, Richmond, Virginia.

Coner, Seldon, to his mother, 8 May 1862. Coner Papers, John Hay Library, Brown University, Providence, Rhode Island.

Douglas, H.T., to S.T.C. Bryan, 29 February 1909. St. George T.C. Bryan Papers, Brockenbrough Library, The Museum of the Confederacy, Richmond, Virginia.

Ewell, Benjamin Stoddert. Papers. Earl Gregg Swem Library, The College of William and Mary, Williamsburg, Virginia.

Furst, Luther. Diary, 16 April 1862, United States Army Military History Institute, Carlisle, Pennsylvania.

Haydon, Charles B. Diary, 7 May 1862. Michigan Historical Collections, Bentley Historical Library, University of Michigan, Ann Arbor, Michigan.

Heintzelman, Samuel Peter. Diary, 6 May 1862, Library of Congress, Washington, D.C.

Hill, D.H., to Longstreet, 31 August 1885. Longstreet Papers, Perkins Library, Duke University, Durham, North Carolina.

Holloway, James Montgomery. Papers, 1861–1905. Virginia Historical Society, Richmond, Virginia.

Hope, James Barron. Papers. Earl Gregg Swem Library, The College of William and Mary, Williamsburg, Virginia.

Jastreminski, Leon, to "Charlie," 2 September 1861. Louisiana State University, Baton Rouge, Louisiana.

Leach, Richard, to his father, 5 February 1862. Leach Papers, Special Collections, William R. Perkins Library, Duke University, Durham, North Carolina.

Leaver, Thomas B. Diary, 2 May 1862. New Hampshire Historical Society.

Lewis, Robert E. Papers. John Moran Quarstein Collection.

Magruder, J.B., to R.E. Lee, 18 June 1861 and 8 August 1861. New York Public Library.

Minnish, J.W. "Reminiscences Relating to the Siege of Yorktown." Virginia War Museum, Newport News, Virginia.

Paris, Comte de. Journal, 12 May 1862, Foundation St. Louis, Paris, France.

Price, R. Channing. Papers. Virginia Historical Society, Richmond.

Sinclair, P.J., to "Alexander," 12 May 1862. North Carolina State Archives, Raleigh.

The Sinking of the Cumberland *by the Ironclad* Merrimac *off Newport News, VA., March 8th, 1862*. Quote from Currier & Ives lithograph. John Moran Quarstein Collection.

Smedlund, William S. "History of the Troup Artillery." Unpublished manuscript. N.p., n.d.

Smith, Benjamin, to R.H. Carnae, 25 August 1861. Louisiana State University, Baton Rouge, Louisiana.

Taliaferro, William Booth. Papers. Earl Gregg Swem Library, The College of William and Mary, Williamsburg, Virginia.

Thompson, Gilbert. Diary. Manuscript Division, Library of Congress, Washington, D.C.

Turner, Vines Edmunds. Papers. Private Collection, North Carolina.

Wise, W.A., to Edward Everett, 19 June 1861. Everett Collection, Massachusetts Historical Society.

BOOKS

Andrews, W.M. *Footprints of a Regiment: A Recollection of the 1st Georgia Regulars*. Atlanta, GA: Longsreet Press, 1992.

Arthur, Robert, and Richard P. Weinert Jr. *Defender of the Chesapeake: The Story of Fort Monroe*. Shippensburg, PA: White Mane Publishing Company, 1989.

Ballentine, George. *Autobiography of an English Soldier in the United States Army Comprising Observations and Adventures in the United States and Mexico*. New York: Stringer and Townsend, 1853.

Balzar, John E., ed. *Buck's Book: A View of the 3rd Vermont Infantry Regiment*. Bolingbrook, IL: Balzar & Associates, 1993.

Barnard, John G. *The Peninsula Campaign and Its Antecedents*. New York: Van Nostrand, 1864.

Benedict, G.G. *Vermont in the Civil War*. Vol. 1. Burlington, VT: Free Press Association, 1886.

Berkley, Henry R. *Four Years in the Confederate Artillery*. Chapel Hill: University of North Carolina Press, 1961.

Blight, David W., ed. *When This Cruel War Is Over: The Civil War Letters of Charles Harvey Brewster*. Amherst: University of Massachusetts Press, 1992.

Brent, Joseph Lancaster. *Memoirs of the War Between the States*. New Orleans, LA: Fontana Printing, 1940.

Bridges, Hal. *Lee's Maverick General: Daniel Harvey Hill*. New York: McGraw Hill, 1961.

Brooke, John M. "The Plan and Construction of the *Merrimac*." *Battles and Leaders of the Civil War*. Vol. 1. Edited by Robert Underwood and Clarence Clough Buel. New York: Century, 1887.

Bruce, Robert V. *Lincoln and the Tools of War*. Indianapolis, IN: Bobbs-Merrill, 1956.

Butler, Benjamin F. *Butler's Book*. Boston, MA: A.M. Thayer & Company, 1892.

Carroll, John M. *Custer in the Civil War, His Unfinished Memoirs*. New York: Stackpole Books, 1976.

Casdorph, Paul D. *Prince John Magruder: His Life and Campaigns*. New York: John Wiley & Sons, 1996.

Catton, Bruce. *The Army of the Potomac: Mr. Lincoln's Army*. New York: Doubleday, 1961.

Cooke, John Esten. *Stonewall Jackson: A Military Biography*. New York: D. Appleton & Company, 1866.

Corell, Philip. *History of the Naval Brigade 99th New York Volunteers Union Coast Guard*. New York: Regiment Veteran Association, 1905.

Corson, William Clark. *My Dear Jennie: A Collection of Love Letters From a Confederate Soldier to His Fiancée During the Period 1861–1865*. Richmond, VA: Dietz Press, 1982.

Crouch, Tim D. *The Eagle Afloat: Two Centuries of the Balloon in America*. Washington, D.C.: Smithsonian Institution, 1983.

Curtis, Richard. *History of the Great Naval Engagement Between the Iron-Clad* Merrimac, *C.S.N., and the* Cumberland, Congress, *and the Iron-Clad* Monitor, *U.S.N., March the 8th and 9th, 1862, As Seen By a Man at the Gun*. N.p.: privately printed, n.d. Reprint, Hampton, VA: Houston Print & Publishing, 1957.

Daly, Robert W. *Aboard the U.S.S.* Monitor, *1862: The Letters of Acting Paymaster William Frederick Keeler*. Annapolis, MD: U.S. Naval Institute, 1964.

Davenport, Alfred. *Camp and Field Life of the Fifth New York Volunteer Infantry*. New York: Dick and Fitzgerald, 1879.

Davis, William C. *Duel Between the First Ironclads*. Baton Rouge: Louisiana State University Press, 1975.

de Joinville, Prince. *The Army of the Potomac: Its Organization, Its Commander, and Its Campaign*. New York: Anson D.F. Randolph, 1862.

de Paris, Comte. *History of the Civil War in America*. Vol. 1. Philadelphia, PA: Jos. H. Coates, 1875.

Donald, David Herbert, ed. *Gone for a Soldier: The Civil War Memoirs of Private Alfred Bellard*. Boston, MA: Little Brown, 1975.

Dougherty, Kevin, and J. Michael Moore. *The Peninsula Campaign of 1862: A Military Analysis*. Jackson: University Press of Mississippi, 2005.

Early, Jubal Anderson. *Narrative of the War Between the States*. New York: De Capo Press, 1991.

Ellis, David R. *The* Monitor *of the Civil War*. N.p.: privately printed, n.d.

Evans, Charles M. *The War of the Aeronauts: A History of Ballooning During the Civil War*. Mechanicsburg, PA: Stackpole Books, 2002.

Faust, Patricia, ed. *Historical Times Illustrated Encyclopedia of the Civil War*. New York: Harper & Row, 1988.

Fox, Gustavus V. *The Confidential Correspondence of Gustavus V. Fox*. New York: Naval Historical Society, 1919.

Freeman, Douglas Southall. *Lee's Lieutenants: A Study in Command.* Vol. 1. New York: Charles Scribner's Sons, 1945.

Gallagher, Gary W., ed. *Fighting for the Confederacy: Personal Recollections of General Edward Porter Alexander.* Chapel Hill: University of North Carolina Press, 1989.

————. *The Richmond Campaign of 1862: The Peninsula & the Seven Days.* Chapel Hill: University of North Carolina Press, 2000.

Greene, Samuel Dana. "In the *Monitor* Turret." *Battles and Leaders of the Civil War.* Vol. 1. Edited by Robert Underwood and Clarence Clough Buel. New York: Century, 1887.

Hannaford, P.A. *The Young Captain Richard C. Derby, Fifteenth Reg. Mass. Volunteers, Who Fell at Antietam.* Boston, MA: Degan, Estes & Company, 1865.

Haskin, William L. *The History of the First Regiment of Artillery from Its Organization in 1821, to 1 January 1875.* Portland, ME: privately printed, 1879.

History of the Twenty-Third Pennsylvania Volunteer Infantry, Birney's Zouaves. Philadelphia, Pennsylvania, 1904.

Hood, John Bell. *Advance and Retreat: Personal Experiences in the United States and Confederate Armies.* New Orleans, LA: Hood Orphan Fund, 1880.

Howe, Henry W. *Passages from the Life of Henry Warren Howe, Consisting of Diary and Letters Written During the Civil War.* Lowell, MA: Courier-Citizen, 1899.

Hudgins, Garland C., and Richard B. Kleese. *Recollections of an Old Dominion Dragoon: Civil War Experiences of Sgt. Robert S. Hudgins, II, Co. B., 3rd Virginia Cavalry.* Orange, VA: Publisher's Press, 1993.

Jensen, Les. *32nd Virginia Infantry.* Lynchburg, VA: H.E. Howard, Inc., 1990.

Johnston, Joseph E. *Narrative of Military Operations During the Civil War.* New York: D. Appleton, 1990.

Jones, Terry L. *Lee's Tigers: The Louisiana Infantry in the Army of Northern Virginia.* Baton Rouge: Louisiana State University Press, 1987.

Keyes, E.D. *Fifty Years' Observation of Men and Events.* New York: Charles Scribner's Sons, 1884.

Lewis, Charles Lee. *Admiral Franklin Buchanan: Fearless Man of Action.* Baltimore, MD: Norman Remington Company, 1929.

Lewis, Samuel. "Life on the *Monitor:* A Seaman's Story of the Fight with the *Merrimac;* Lively Experiences Inside the Famous 'Cheesebox on a Raft.'" *Campfire Sketches and Battlefield Echoes of '61–'65.* Edited by William C. King and William P. Derby. Springfield, MA: 1883.

Lyons, Patrick. *A Soldier's Log.* Providence, RI: privately printed, 1988.

McArthur, Judith N., and Orville Vernon Burton, eds. *A Gentleman and an Officer: A Military and Social History of James B. Griffin's Civil War.* New York: Oxford University Press, 1996.

McCash, William B. *Thomas R.R. Cobb: The Making of a Southern Nationalist.* Macon, GA: Mercer University Press, 1983.

McClellan, George Brinton. *Report on the Organization of the Army of the Potomac, and of Its Campaigns in Virginia and Maryland.* Washington, D.C.: Government Printing Office, 1864.

————. *George B. McClellan's Own Story.* New York: Charles L. Webster, 1887.

McMurry, Richard M. *John Bell Hood and the War for Southern Independence.* Lexington: University Press of Kentucky, 1982.

Miller, William J., ed. *The Peninsula Campaign of 1862.* Vols. 1–4. Campbell, CA: Savas Publishing Company, 1995–98.

Moore, Robert H., II. *Miscellaneous Disbanded Virginia Light Artillery.* Lynchburg, VA: H.E. Howard, Inc., 1997.

Nanzig, Thomas P. *3rd Virginia Cavalry.* Lynchburg, VA: H.E. Howard, Inc., 1989.

Norton, Oliver Willcox. *Army Letters: 1861–1865.* Chicago, IL: privately printed, 1903.

O'Brien, John Emmett. *Telegraphing in Battle.* Scranton, PA: privately printed, 1910.

Oeffinger, John C. *A Soldier's Journal: The Civil War Letters of Major General Lafayette McLaws.* Chapel Hill: University of North Carolina Press, 2002.

Official Records of the Union and Confederate Navies in the War of the Rebellion. 30 vols. Washington, D.C.: Government Printing Office, 1894–1922.

Osborne, William M. *History of the Twenty-ninth Regiment of Massachusetts.* Boston, MA: J. Putnam, 1877.

Palfrey, Francis W. *The Peninsular Campaign of General McClellan in 1862.* Boston: Military and Historical Society of Massachusetts, 1881.

Parker, William M. *Recollections of a Naval Officer, 1844–1865.* New York: Charles Scribner's Sons, 1883.

Patterson, Edmund. *Yankee Rebel: The Civil War Journal of Edmund Dewitt Patterson.* Chapel Hill: University of North Carolina Press, 1966.

Perry, Milton F. *Infernal Machines: The Story of Confederate Submarines and Mine Warfare.* Baton Rouge: Louisiana State Press, 1965.

Quarstein, John V. *Big Bethel: The First Battle.* Charleston, SC: The History Press, 2011.

———. *The Civil War on the Peninsula.* Charleston, SC: Arcadia Publishing, 1997.

———. *CSS* Virginia: *Sink Before Surrender.* Charleston, SC: The History Press, 2012.

———. *Hampton and Newport News in the Civil War.* Lynchburg, VA: H.E. Howard, Inc., 1998.

———. *The* Monitor *Boys: The Crew of the Union's First Ironclad.* Charleston, SC: The History Press, 2011.

Reaney, Henry. "How the Gun-Boat *Zouave* Aided the *Congress.*" *Battles and Leaders of the Civil War.* Vol. 1. Edited by Robert Underwood and Clarence Clough Buel. New York: Century, 1887.

Reid, J.W. *History of the Fourth Regiment of S.C. Volunteers.* Greenville, SC: Shannon & Company, 1892.

Rhodes, Robert Hunt, ed. *All for the Union: The Civil War Diary and Letters of Elisha Hunt Rhodes.* Lincoln, RI: Andrew Mobray, 1985.

Ritchie, Norman L., ed. *Four Years in the First New York Light Artillery: The Papers of David F. Ritchie.* Hamilton, NY: Edmonston, 1997.

Robertson, Elizabeth Whitley, ed. *Weep Not for Me, Dear Mother: The War Experiences of Private Eli Pinson Landers of the 16th Regiment Georgia Volunteers, The Flint Hill Grays.* Washington, GA: Venture Press, 1991.

Rosenblatt, Emil, and Ruth Rosenblatt, eds. *Hard Marching Every Day: The Civil War Letters of Private Wilbur Fiske, 1861–1865.* Lawrence: University Press of Kansas, 1992.

Sears, Stephen W. *George B. McClellan, the Young Napoleon.* New York: Ticknor & Fields, 1988.

————. *To the Gates of Richmond*. New York: Ticknor & Fields, 1992.

Sears, Stephen W., ed. *The Civil War Papers of George B. McClellan*. New York: Ticknor & Fields, 1989.

Selfridge, Thomas O., Jr. *Memoirs of Thomas O. Selfridge, Jr., Rear Admiral, U.S.N.* New York: G.P. Putnam's Sons, 1924.

Settles, Thomas M. *John Bankhead Magruder: A Military Reappraisal*. Baton Rouge: Louisiana State University Press, 2009.

Smith, William F. *Autobiography of Major General William F. Smith, 1861–1865*. Dayton, OH: Morningside Press, 1990.

Sneden, Robert Knox. *Eye of the Storm: A Civil War Odyssey*. Edited by Charles F. Bryan and Nelson D. Lankford. New York: Simon & Schuster, 2000.

Sorrel, G. Moxley. *Reflections of a Confederate Staff Officer*. New York and Washington: Neale Publishing, 1905.

Squires, W.H.T. *Unleashed at Long Last*. Portsmouth, VA: privately printed, 1939.

Steiner, Paul E. *Disease in the Civil War: Natural Biological Warfare in 1861–1865*. Springfield, IL: Charles C. Thomas Publishers, 1968.

Stevens, George T. *Three Years in the Sixth Corps*. New York: Van Nostrand, 1870.

Stiles, Robert. *Four Years Under Marse Robert*. New York: Neale, 1903.

Still, William N., Jr. *Iron Afloat*. Columbia: University of South Carolina Press, 1985.

Stuyvesant, Moses S. "How the *Cumberland* Went Down." *War Papers and Personal Reminiscences, 1861–1865*. Vol. 1. Wilmington, NC: Barefoot Publications Company, 1992.

Styple, William B., ed. *Letters from the Peninsula: The Civil War Letters of General Philip Kearny*. Kearney, NJ: Belle Grove Press, 1988.

————. *Writing & Fighting from the Army of Northern Virginia*. Kearney, NJ: Belle Grove Press, 2003.

U.S. Congress, Senate 1, 1848.

Wainwright, Charles S. *A Diary of Battle: The Personal Journals of Colonel Charles S. Wainwright, 1861–1865*. New York: Harcourt, Brace & World, 1962.

Waite, Otis F.R. *Vermont in the Great Rebellion*. Claremont, VT: Tracy, Chase and Company, 1869.

War of the Rebellion: A Compilation of the Official Records of the Union and Confederate Armies. 130 vols. Washington, D.C.: Government Printing Office, 1889–1901.

Webb, Alexander S. *The Peninsula*. New York: Charles Scribner's Sons, 1881.

West, George Benjamin. *When the Yankees Came*. Richmond, VA: Dietz Press, 1977.

Weymouth, A.B., ed. *A Memorial Sketch of Lieut. Edgar M. Newcomb of the Nineteenth Mass. Vols*. Malden, MA: Alvin G. Brown, 1883.

White, William S. *A Diary of the War, Or What I Saw of It*. Richmond, VA: privately printed, 1983.

Wood, John Taylor. "The First Fight of Iron-clads." *Battles and Leaders of the Civil War*. Vol. 1. Edited by Robert Underwood and Clarence Clough Buel. New York: Century, 1887.

Woodward, C. Vann, ed. *Mary Chesnut's Civil War*. New Haven, CT: Yale University Press, 1981.

BIBLIOGRAPHY

PERIODICALS

Adams, Ida Bright, ed. "Letters of James Rush Holmes." *Western Pennsylvania Historical Magazine* 22 (June 1961).

Alger, F.S. "*Congress* and the *Merrimac*." *New England Magazine* 14 (February 1899).

Bradley, Chester D. "The *Fanny*: First Aircraft Carrier." *Casemate Chronicles* 2 (1968).

Brown, Walter, J., ed. "Benjamin Huskee's Letter from Bethel." *Civil War Times Illustrated* (October 1961).

Bryan, John Randolph. "Balloon Used for Scout Duty in C.S.A." *Southern Historical Society Papers* 33 (April 1914). Richmond, Virginia.

Cline, William R. "The Ironclad Ram *Virginia*." *Southern Historical Society Papers* 32 (1904).

Coner, Forrest, P., ed. "Letters of Lieutenant Robert M. Miller to His Family, 1861–1862." *Virginia Magazine of History and Biography* 70 (January 1962).

Custer, George Armstrong. "War Memories." *The Galaxy—A Magazine of Entertaining Reading* 22 (November 1876).

Daily Richmond Enquirer, 22 April 1861.

Davis, Emma-Jo L. "Mulberry Island and the Civil War, April 1861–May 1862." *Quarterly Bulletin* (March 1968). Fort Eustis Archaeological Society.

Denkins, James. "The Battle of Big Bethel, VA." *Confederate Veteran* 26 (1918).

Eggleston, John R. "Captain Eggleston's Narrative of the Battle of the *Merrimac*." *Southern Historical Society Papers* 41 (September 1916).

Eisenberg, Albert C. "The 3rd Vermont Has Won a Name: Corporal George Q. French's Account of the Battle of Lee's Mills, Virginia." *Vermont History* 49 (Fall 1981).

Greene, Samuel Dana. "I Fired the First Gun and Thus Commenced the Great Battle." *American Heritage* 8 (June 1957).

Haw, Joseph R. "The Burning of Hampton." *Confederate Veteran* 32 (October 1924).

Hord, B.M. "The Battle of Big Bethel, VA." *Confederate Veteran* 26 (1918).

Jones, Catesby ap Roger. "Services of the *Virginia*." *Southern Historical Society Papers* 11 (January 1883).

Lee, Baker P. "Magruder's Peninsula Campaign in 1862." *Southern Historical Society Papers* 19 (1891).

Littlepage, Hardin B. "Statement of Midshipman Littlepage." *Southern Historical Society Papers* 11 (1883).

Long, A.L. "Memoir of General John Bankhead Magruder." *Southern Historical Society Papers* 12 (1884).

Maury, Richard L. "The Battle of Williamsburg and the Charge of the Twenty-Fourth Virginia of Early's Brigade." *Southern Historical Society Papers* (1880).

New York Illustrated News, 14 October 1861.

New York Sun, 28 February 1897.

New York Times, 2 May 1861, 14 June 1861 and 9 August 1861.

Noyles, G.B., ed. "Letters Written by Sgt. George B. Noyles, Co. K, 11th Regiment Maine Volunteers During the Civil War." *Island Advantages* 27 (June 1962).

Peirce, Edmond L. "The Contrabands at Fortress Monroe." *Atlantic Monthly* (November 1861).

Phillips, Dinwiddie. "The Career of the Iron-Clad *Virginia*." *Collections of the Virginia Historical Society* 6 (1887).

Rae, Thomas W. "The Little *Monitor* Saved Our Lives." *American History Illustrated* 1 (18 July 1966).

Ramsay, H. Aston. "The Most Famous of Sea Duels: The Story of the *Merrimac*'s Engagement with the *Monitor*, and the Events that Preceded and Followed the Fight, Told by a Survivor." *Harper's Weekly*, 10 February 1912.

Richmond Daily Examiner, 22 April 1861, 12 August 1861 and 3 April 1862.

Richmond Dispatch, 8 June 1861, 24 June 1861, 26 June 1861 and 10 July 1861.

Stimers, Alban C. "An Engineer Aboard the *Monitor*." *Civil War Times Illustrated* 9 (April 1970).

Tindall, William. "True Story of the *Virginia*." *Virginia Magazine of History and Biography* 31 (January 1923).

Williams, Asher. "Letters from a Soldier in the Union Army." *The Staten Island Historian* 15 (April–June 1961).

Wilson, Gary, ed. "The Diary of John S. Tucker: Confederate Soldier from Alabama." *Alabama Historical Quarterly* 43 (Spring 1981).

Index

About the Authors

JOHN V. QUARSTEIN is an award-winning historian, preservationist, lecturer and author. He served as director of the Virginia War Museum for more than thirty years and, after retirement, continues to work as a historian for the city of Newport News. He is in demand as a speaker throughout the nation. Quarstein is the author of fifteen books, including *The CSS* Virginia*: Sink Before Surrender* and *Big Bethel: The First Battle.* He has produced, narrated and written several PBS documentaries, including the film series *Civil War in Hampton Roads*, a 2007 Silver Telly Award winner. John is the recipient of the Society for History in the Federal Government's 2011 Henry Adams Prize for his book *The* Monitor *Boys: The Crew of the Union's First Ironclads.* He also received the 1993 President's Award for Historic Preservation and the United Daughters of the Confederacy's 1999 Jefferson Davis Gold Medal. Besides his lifelong interest in Tidewater Virginia's Civil War experience, Quarstein is an avid duck hunter and decoy collector. He lives on Old Point Comfort in Hampton, Virginia, and on his family's Eastern Shore farm near Chestertown, Maryland.

J. MICHAEL MOORE is the curator and registrar for Lee Hall Mansion and Endview Plantation in Newport News, Virginia. He received a bachelor of arts in history from Christopher Newport University and a master of arts in history from Old Dominion University. While earning his graduate degree, he taught American history at ODU. Since his employment with the City of Newport News, Moore has curated exhibits at historic sites and led battlefield tours throughout Maryland, North Carolina, Virginia and West Virginia. He is also a consultant with the Maritime Archaeological and Historical Society, the Isle of Wight County Historic Resources and the York County Historical Museum. In addition, Moore serves on the Civil War Sesquicentennial Committees for the city of Newport News, York County and Williamsburg/James City County. He is a lecturer for Christopher Newport University's LifeLong Learning Society. Moore is co-author with Kevin Dougherty of *The Peninsula Campaign of 1862: A Military Analysis*. Michael has also served as editor and photographic editor for eleven books and written articles for *Virginia Cavalcade*, *North & South* and *Military Collector & Historian*. A native of Newport News, Moore lives in Yorktown, Virginia.